I0017976

The Linux Administrator's Handbook: A Practical Guide to Mastery

Sarful Hassan

Preface

Who This Book Is For

This book is for anyone seeking to build or enhance Linux system administration skills, from beginners to IT professionals preparing for certifications.

How This Book Is Organized

The book covers 17 chapters, starting with basics like setup and file system management, progressing to advanced topics such as security, automation, and cloud administration. Each chapter includes practical examples and exercises.

What Was Left Out

This book focuses on general-purpose administration tasks and widely used tools, omitting niche topics like kernel development.

Code Style (About the Code)

Code examples follow a clear, readable style for easy use in the Linux terminal. Annotations explain key commands and scripts.

Release Notes

This first edition reflects the latest best practices in Linux administration and includes updated content on security, automation, and cloud technologies.

Notes on the First Edition

The first edition is based on practical experience and real-world scenarios. Feedback for improvement is welcome.

MechatronicsLAB Online Learning

- **Email:** mechatronicslab@gmail.com
- **Website:** mechatronicslab.net

Acknowledgments for the First Edition

Special thanks to the MechatronicsLAB team, reviewers, and beta readers whose support made this book possible.

Copyright

Disclaimer

The information is for educational purposes only. The author and publisher are not responsible for errors, omissions, or damages resulting from its use. Test configurations in a safe environment before production deployment.

Chapter 1: Introduction to Linux Administration

Chapter Overview

To make Linux administration accessible for absolute beginners, this chapter introduces concepts with simplified explanations and real-world relevance. Each section includes practical examples to help readers connect theory to practice. Common beginner mistakes are highlighted with solutions, ensuring learners avoid pitfalls early on. Additionally, practical exercises are included to reinforce learning through hands-on practice.

- **The Importance of Understanding Linux Administration**
    - Linux administration forms the backbone of modern IT infrastructure, ensuring systems run smoothly and efficiently.
    - This chapter lays the groundwork for mastering Linux by introducing fundamental concepts and responsibilities.
- **How This Chapter Prepares You for the Rest of the Book**
    - Provides an understanding of what Linux administration entails.
    - Introduces key skills and tools needed to progress through advanced topics.
    - Offers exercises to practice foundational tasks like creating a user or checking system performance.

The Role of a System Administrator

- **Managing System Resources: CPU, Memory, and Disk**
    - Balancing resource allocation to avoid bottlenecks.
    - Monitoring resource usage to identify inefficiencies.
    - Example: Use free -m to view memory usage and df -h to check disk space.
- **Monitoring System Performance**
    - Using tools like top, htop, and vmstat to gauge system health.
    - Setting alerts for unusual system behavior.
    - Example: Run top to view active processes and sort by memory usage.

- **Troubleshooting and Resolving Issues**
  - Diagnosing and fixing software and hardware problems.
  - Maintaining system logs for proactive problem-solving.
  - Tip: Use journalctl to review logs for systemd services.
- **Managing Users, Groups, and Permissions**
  - Ensuring secure access by assigning appropriate permissions.
  - Using tools like usermod, groupadd, and chmod effectively.
  - Practice: Create a new user and assign them to a group.

Key Characteristics of Linux Administration

- **Open Source Nature: Flexibility and Customization**
  - Modify and adapt the system to specific organizational needs.
  - Access to an extensive community and collaborative development.
- **Stability and Security as Key Features**
  - High reliability for critical applications.
  - Robust built-in security features and regular updates.
  - Real-World Example: How Linux supports high-availability services in web hosting.
- **Importance in Modern IT Infrastructure**
  - Integral to cloud computing, web hosting, and enterprise systems.
  - Provides a foundation for DevOps, AI, and edge computing.

What is Linux Administration?

- **Definition and Core Objectives**
  - The practice of managing Linux systems to ensure they operate reliably and securely.
  - Includes tasks such as installing software, configuring networks, and managing security.
- **How Linux Differs from Other Operating Systems**
  - Open-source architecture with unparalleled flexibility.
  - Command-line driven, providing direct control over the system.

- o Interactive Example: Compare ls commands in Linux vs. GUI file explorers in Windows.
- **Typical Tasks and Responsibilities**
  - o System updates and patches.
  - o User account and permission management.
  - o Network and storage configuration.

Role of a System Administrator

- **Ensuring System Availability and Reliability**
  - o Planning for uptime and redundancy.
  - o Performing regular backups and failover testing.
  - o Hands-On Task: Schedule a simple backup using rsync.
- **Implementing Security Measures**
  - o Configuring firewalls and intrusion detection systems.
  - o Enforcing access control policies.
  - o Real-World Scenario: Setting up ufw to allow SSH access only.
- **Overseeing Network and Storage Solutions**
  - o Setting up network interfaces and VPNs.
  - o Managing partitions and logical volumes for storage.

Key Skills and Responsibilities

- **Proficiency with Command-Line Tools**
  - o Mastering tools like grep, awk, sed, and vi.
  - o Understanding shell scripting for automation.
  - o Tip: Practice editing files with nano before transitioning to vi.
- **Understanding Networking Concepts**
  - o Familiarity with IP addressing, DNS, and routing.
  - o Configuring services like SSH and FTP.
  - o Activity: Test connectivity using ping and troubleshoot with traceroute.
- **Scripting for Automation**
  - o Writing Bash scripts to automate repetitive tasks.
  - o Scheduling tasks using cron and at.
  - o Example Script: Create a script to clean up temporary files.

- **Collaboration with Development Teams**
  - Facilitating CI/CD pipelines.
  - Supporting developers with system resources and configurations.

Why Choose Linux for Administration?

- **Popularity in Enterprises**
  - Powers most servers and cloud platforms.
  - Widely used in data centers and supercomputers.
- **Open Source Advantages**
  - **Community-Driven Support**: Active forums and contributions from developers worldwide.
  - **Cost Effectiveness**: Free software without licensing fees.
  - **Transparency and Customizability**: Ability to audit code and tailor the system to needs.
  - Practical Insight: Discuss how open-source tools like Docker integrate seamlessly with Linux.

Structure of This Book

- **Overview of Chapters and Topics**
  - Setting Up a Linux Environment: Choosing distributions and initial setup.
  - Managing File Systems and Users: Core administration tasks.
  - Advanced Topics like Virtualization and Scripting: Going beyond the basics.
  - Practical Tips for Security and Monitoring: Ensuring reliability and safety.
- **How to Navigate and Use the Book Effectively**
  - Follow chapters sequentially for a comprehensive understanding.
  - Refer to specific sections for quick problem-solving and guidance.
  - Suggested Reading Order: Begin with basic concepts, then progress to hands-on activities.

Chapter 2: Setting Up Your Linux Environment

Chapter Overview

This chapter is designed to help you, even if you are completely new to Linux, set up your environment step-by-step. You will learn how to pick the right Linux version, install it on your computer, and configure basic settings. Each section is written in simple terms, with examples and detailed explanations to ensure a thorough understanding. Practical tips and troubleshooting steps are also included to guide you through the process.

The Role of a Linux Environment Setup

- **Foundation for Linux Usage**: Setting up a Linux environment is the first step in using Linux effectively.
- **Choosing the Right Distribution**: Select a Linux version (distribution) that suits your goals and experience.
- **Installing the System**: Perform the installation on your computer.
- **Configuring the System**: Adjust settings to ensure smooth, secure, and efficient operation.
- **Outcome**: A properly set up Linux environment lays the groundwork for all future tasks.

Key Characteristics of Different Distributions

Linux offers many versions (distributions), each tailored for specific purposes. Selecting the right one depends on your experience level and goals.

- **What is a Linux Distribution?**

A Linux distribution is an operating system that bundles the Linux kernel with essential tools and software to create a complete platform for various tasks. It provides the foundation for all applications and services running on the system.

Distribution	Features	Best For
Ubuntu	User-friendly, easy to install, large community support	Beginners
CentOS	Stable, long-term support, suitable for enterprise use	Business and server environments
Fedora	Cutting-edge features, frequent updates	Developers and advanced users

- **Factors to Consider for Beginners**
  - Ease of Use: Is it simple to navigate? Ubuntu is highly recommended for new users.
  - Support: Does it have good documentation and an active community?
  - Software Compatibility: Does it support the applications you need?
  - Security: Is it reliable and well-maintained?

Common Beginner Mistakes

1. **Skipping System Requirements**:
   - Not checking if your computer meets the minimum hardware requirements can lead to installation failures.
   - **Tip**: Look up the hardware requirements for your chosen distribution before starting.
2. **Forgetting to Back Up Data**:
   - Installing Linux can erase existing data if done incorrectly.
   - **Warning**: Always back up your files to an external drive before beginning.
3. **Misconfiguring Partitions**:
   - Selecting "Erase Disk" during installation without understanding its impact will delete everything.
   - **Tip**: Use the "Manual Partitioning" option if you have existing data to preserve.
4. **Network Configuration Errors**:
   - Setting incorrect IP addresses can disconnect your system from the network.
   - **Tip**: Double-check all network settings, and test

connectivity with ping.

Simplify Advanced Concepts

- **Partition Types Analogy**:
  - Think of your hard drive as a library. Primary partitions are the main bookshelves, extended partitions are additional shelves, and logical partitions are smaller sections on those shelves.
  - **Tip**: Beginners should use the guided partitioning option during installation.
- **Static vs. Dynamic IP Addressing**:
  - A static IP is like a reserved parking spot—it never changes. A dynamic IP is like general parking—it changes every time you park.
  - **Tip**: Use a static IP only if setting up a server.

Highlight Key Tools for Beginners

1. **Rufus**: A tool to create bootable USB drives for installing Linux.
   - **Why Use It**: Converts ISO images into bootable USB drives.
   - **Note**: Available for Windows users and easy to operate.
2. **GParted**: A graphical tool for partition management.
   - **Why Use It**: Helps you resize, delete, or create partitions visually.
   - **Warning**: Double-check changes before applying them to avoid data loss.
3. **Ping Command**: Tests network connectivity.
   - **Why Use It**: Quickly identifies if a system is reachable.
   - **Example**: Run ping 8.8.8.8 to test internet connectivity.

Add Practical Scenarios

1. **Testing Linux via Live Environment**:
   - Before installing, use a live session to explore Linux without making permanent changes.
   - **Tip**: Boot from the USB and choose the "Try" option.
2. **Setting Up a Home Server**:
   - Install Ubuntu Server to host a personal website or file server.
   - **Note**: Start with minimal installation and add Apache or

Nginx as needed.

3. **Dual-Boot Setup**:
   - Install Linux alongside Windows for flexibility.
   - **Warning**: Use manual partitioning to allocate space safely for both systems.

Choosing the Right Distribution for Administration

Distribution	Advantages	Suitable For
CentOS	Stability, long-term support, ideal for businesses	Business and enterprise servers
Ubuntu Server	Beginner-friendly, excellent community support	Beginners and general use
Red Hat Enterprise	Robust security and performance, professional support	Enterprises needing premium support

Installation and Initial Configuration

This section guides you through the key steps to install and configure your Linux system effectively. It provides a clear breakdown for beginners, ensuring that each task is straightforward and manageable.

Step 1: Understanding Installation Types

- **Server Installation**:
  - Minimal installation for maximum performance.
  - Operated via the command line (no graphical interface by default).
- **Desktop Installation**:
  - Includes a graphical user interface (GUI) for easier interaction.
  - Preinstalled applications like browsers and office tools are included.

Step 2: Preparing for Installation

- Verify hardware compatibility (processor, RAM, and storage).
  - **Tip**: Refer to your distribution's official website for specific requirements.
- Backup existing data to prevent accidental loss.
  - **Warning**: Proceeding without a backup risks losing important files.

Step 3: Setting Up the Partition Scheme

- **Types of Partitions: Primary, Extended, Logical**:
  - **Primary**: The main areas for storing data, limited to four per drive.
  - **Extended**: Allows additional partitions beyond the four primary ones.
  - **Logical**: Smaller sections within an extended partition.
- **Guided vs. Manual Partitioning**:
  - Guided: Automatically sets up partitions, ideal for beginners.
  - Manual: Offers complete control, best for experienced users.
  - **Tip**: Use the guided option unless you need custom configurations.

Understanding Installation Types: Server vs. Desktop

- **Server Installation**:
  - Minimal installation for maximum performance.
  - Operated via the command line (no graphical interface by default).
- **Desktop Installation**:
  - Includes a graphical user interface (GUI) for easier interaction.
  - Preinstalled applications like browsers and office tools are included.

Preparing for Installation: Checking System Requirements

- Verify hardware compatibility (processor, RAM, and storage).
  - **Tip**: Refer to your distribution's official website for specific requirements.
- Backup existing data to prevent accidental loss.
  - **Warning**: Proceeding without a backup risks losing important files.

Setting Up the Partition Scheme

- **Types of Partitions: Primary, Extended, Logical**:
  - **Primary**: The main areas for storing data, limited to four per drive.
  - **Extended**: Allows additional partitions beyond the four

primary ones.

- o **Logical**: Smaller sections within an extended partition.
- **Guided vs. Manual Partitioning**:
  - o Guided: Automatically sets up partitions, ideal for beginners.
  - o Manual: Offers complete control, best for experienced users.
  - o **Tip**: Use the guided option unless you need custom configurations.

Configuring Basic System Settings
- **Setting Up the Hostname**:
  - o A hostname identifies your computer on a network.
  - o Example: myserver.localdomain
  - o **Tip**: Choose a clear and meaningful name for easy identification.
- **Adjusting Keyboard Layout and Language**:
  - o Select the layout and language that match your location.
  - o Example: US English or UK English.
  - o **Note**: This can be changed later if needed.

Network Settings
- **Introduction to IP Addressing**:
  - o IP addresses are unique identifiers for devices on a network.
  - o Types: IPv4 (e.g., 192.168.1.1) and IPv6 (e.g., 2001:0db8::1).
- **Static vs. Dynamic IPs**:
  - o Static IPs are manually set and do not change.
  - o Dynamic IPs are automatically assigned by a DHCP server.
  - o Example: Edit /etc/netplan/ in Ubuntu to configure a static IP.
  - o **Tip**: Use dynamic IPs for personal use and static IPs for servers.

Timezone and Locale Configuration
- **Selecting Time Zones for Beginners**:
  - o Use the command timedatectl set-timezone <Region>/<City> to set the correct timezone.

- o Example: timedatectl set-timezone America/New_York sets the timezone to New York.
  - o **Tip**: Run timedatectl to confirm that the timezone is configured correctly.
- **Setting Locale Preferences**:
  - o Locales determine the language and regional settings like date formats.
  - o Use the command sudo locale-gen <locale> to generate the required locale.
    - Example: sudo locale-gen en_US.UTF-8 generates the US English locale.
  - o Apply the locale settings with sudo update-loca e LANG=<locale>.
    - Example: sudo update-locale LANG=en_US.UTF-8 sets the US English locale as default.
  - o **Note**: Use locale to check the active locale settings on your system.

By the end of this chapter, you will have a fully operational Linux environment tailored to your needs. This environment will be ready for further customization, making it a solid foundation for exploring advanced Linux features and functionalities. Remember, each step is crucial for creating a reliable and efficient system, so take your time and refer back to the guide as needed.

Chapter 3: Linux File System Management

Chapter Overview
This chapter delves into the essential concepts of Linux file system management. It provides a comprehensive guide on understanding the Linux file system hierarchy, the roles of critical directories, and step-by-step instructions for managing file systems, partitions, and logical volumes. With practical examples and detailed explanations, this chapter equips you with the knowledge to navigate and configure Linux file systems effectively.

The Role of File System Management
- **Efficient Data Organization**: Prevents fragmentation and improves overall system performance.
- **Optimized Storage Utilization**: Assigns appropriate file systems (e.g., ext4 for general use, xfs for large files) based on storage needs.
- **System Stability**: Maintains integrity and ensures reliable operation by properly managing file systems.
- **Custom Configuration**: Enables the creation of file systems tailored to specific purposes.
- **Integration into Directory Tree**: Configures mounting points to incorporate file systems seamlessly.
- **Proactive Monitoring**: Detects and resolves storage issues to avoid disruptions.

Key Characteristics of Linux File Systems
Linux file systems are robust, flexible, and designed for diverse workloads. Understanding their features allows administrators to maximize performance and reliability.

Understanding the Linux File System Hierarchy
The Linux file system hierarchy is structured according to the Filesystem Hierarchy Standard (FHS), ensuring consistency across distributions. It organizes data into directories based on their purpose.

- **What is a File System?**
  - A file system defines how data is stored, retrieved, and managed on storage devices.
  - Common file systems: ext4 (default), xfs (for large files), and btrfs (supports snapshots).
- **Overview of Filesystem Hierarchy Standard (FHS)**
  - The FHS standardizes the directory structure to simplify navigation and system management.

Directory	Description
/etc	Configuration files for system and applications (e.g., /etc/passwd).
/var	Variable data files like logs, caches, and databases (e.g., /var/log).
/usr	User applications and utilities (e.g., /usr/bin for executables).
/bin	Essential binaries (e.g., ls, cat).
/sbin	Administrative binaries (e.g., fsck, reboot).
/home	User home directories (e.g., /home/username).
/root	Home directory for the root user.
/dev	Device files representing hardware components (e.g., /dev/sda1).
/tmp	Temporary files created by applications.

- **Importance of /etc, /var, and /usr**
  - **/etc**: Central repository for configuration, essential for system and application setup.
  - **/var**: Stores dynamic data like logs, ensuring system health monitoring.
  - **/usr**: Hosts user-installed software and libraries, critical for expanding functionality.

Managing File Systems and Mount Points

Real-Life Example

- **Scenario**: You attach a new external hard drive to your system and want to use it as a backup drive.

- Step 1: Connect the drive and find its device name using lsblk (e.g., /dev/sdb1).
- Step 2: Mount the drive temporarily: sudo mount /dev/sdb1 /mnt/backup.
- Step 3: Add a permanent entry in /etc/fstab for automatic mounting.
- **Solution**: Use mount -a to test the entry and ensure the drive mounts correctly after reboot.

Common Mistakes Section

1. **Editing /etc/fstab Incorrectly**:
   - Mistake: Using invalid syntax or incorrect device names.
   - Solution: Test changes with sudo mount -a before rebooting to prevent boot errors.
2. **Unmounting a Busy File System**:
   - Mistake: Trying to unmount a file system in use by applications.
   - Solution: Use lsof | grep /mountpoint to identify processes using the mount and terminate them before unmounting.
3. **Forgetting to Create a Mount Point**:
   - Mistake: Attempting to mount a file system to a non-existent directory.
   - Solution: Always create the mount point first with mkdir /mnt/mountpoint.
- **Note**: Always ensure the file system is not in use before unmounting to prevent data loss.
- **Warning**: Incorrect fstab entries can render the system unbootable. Always test with mount -a after making changes.

What is Mounting in Linux?
   - Mounting attaches a file system to a directory, making it accessible to users and applications.
- **Mounting and Unmounting File Systems**
   - Use sudo mount to attach and sudo umount to safely detach file systems.
- **Using the mount Command**
   - Example: sudo mount /dev/sdX1 /mnt mounts a partition

to /mnt.
- **Temporary vs. Permanent Mounts**
  - Temporary mounts last until the system reboots.
  - Permanent mounts are defined in /etc/fstab for persistence.
- **Configuring /etc/fstab**
  - **Understanding fstab Entries:**
    - Example: /dev/sdX1 /mnt ext4 defaults 0 0.
  - **Testing New Entries:**
    - Run sudo mount -a to apply and validate /etc/fstab changes.

Disk Partitioning and Formatting
Real-Life Example
- **Scenario:** You are setting up a dual-boot system with Linux and Windows.
  - Step 1: Use Windows Disk Management to shrink an existing partition and create free space.
  - Step 2: Boot into a Linux live environment and use fdisk or parted to create new partitions in the free space.
  - Step 3: Format the partitions with appropriate file systems (e.g., ext4 for Linux, NTFS for shared storage).
  - **Solution:** Ensure proper partitioning and labeling to avoid overwriting critical data.

Common Mistakes Section
1. **Choosing the Wrong Partition Type:**
   - Mistake: Selecting MBR instead of GPT for modern systems.
   - Solution: Use parted to initialize disks with GPT for systems requiring large storage or UEFI boot.
2. **Formatting the Wrong Partition:**
   - Mistake: Accidentally formatting the wrong device.
   - Solution: Double-check the device name with lsblk or fdisk -l before running formatting commands.

3. **Not Aligning Partitions Properly**:
   - o Mistake: Misaligned partitions can cause performance issues.
   - o Solution: Use parted with the align-check command to ensure proper alignment.
- **Note**: Use fdisk for simple tasks and parted for advanced configurations, especially on GPT disks.
- **Warning**: Partitioning and formatting will erase all data on the selected disk. Double-check the device before proceeding.
- **What is Disk Partitioning?**
   - o Divides a storage device into segments to organize and allocate space efficiently.
- **Tools for Partitioning: fdisk vs. parted**

Tool	Description	Suitable For
fdisk	Command-line tool for basic partitioning.	Simple tasks and MBR disks.
parted	Advanced tool for modern layouts, supports GPT.	Complex tasks and large disks.

- **Using fdisk for Basic Partitioning**
   - o Commands:
     - ▪ n: Create a new partition.
     - ▪ d: Delete a partition.
     - ▪ p: Print the partition table.
   - o Example: sudo fdisk /dev/sdX.
- **Using parted for Advanced Partitioning**
   - o Commands:
     - ▪ mklabel gpt: Set partition table to GPT.
     - ▪ mkpart: Create a partition.
   - o Example: sudo parted /dev/sdX.
- **Formatting Partitions with mkfs**
   - o Command: sudo mkfs.ext4 /dev/sdX1 formats with ext4.

Filesystem	Description	Best Use Case
ext4	Reliable, default in most Linux distributions.	General-purpose workloads.
xfs	High-performance, handles large files efficiently.	Data-heavy applications, databases.
btrfs	Advanced features like snapshots and pooling.	Advanced setups, dynamic scaling.

Logical Volumes (LVM): Creating and Resizing
Real-Life Example

- **Scenario**: You have a database application requiring additional storage without downtime.
  - o Step 1: Add a new disk to the system and initialize it as a physical volume: sudo pvcreate /dev/sdc.
  - o Step 2: Extend the existing volume group: sudo vgextend vg_name /dev/sdc.
  - o Step 3: Increase the logical volume size: sudo lvextend -L +50G /dev/vg_name/lv_name.
  - o Step 4: Resize the file system to use the expanded space.
  - o **Solution**: Use file system-specific tools like resize2fs or xfs_growfs to make additional space available.

Common Mistakes Section

1. **Extending a Logical Volume Without Resizing the File System**:
   - o Mistake: Increasing the LV size but forgetting to expand the file system.
   - o Solution: Always run the appropriate resize command for the file system after extending the LV.
2. **Not Backing Up Data Before Resizing**:
   - o Mistake: Resizing logical volumes without a backup can result in data loss if errors occur.
   - o Solution: Always perform a backup using tools like rsync before making changes.
3. **Over-Allocating Volume Group Space**:
   - o Mistake: Assigning all available space to a single logical volume, leaving none for future expansion.

- o Solution: Plan allocations carefully, reserving some free space for future needs.
- **Note**: Logical Volumes allow dynamic resizing, making them ideal for systems with changing storage requirements.
- **Warning**: Always back up data before resizing volumes to avoid accidental data loss.

What is LVM?
- o Logical Volume Manager (LVM) provides flexible disk management by abstracting storage into logical volumes.
- **Steps to Create a Logical Volume**

0.   Initialize a physical volume: sudo pvcreate /dev/sdX.

1.   Create a volume group: sudo vgcreate vg_name /dev/sdX.

2.   Create a logical volume: sudo lvcreate -L 10G -n lv_name vg_name.

- **Resizing Logical Volumes Safely**
  - o Increase size: sudo lvextend -L +5G /dev/vg_name/lv_name.
  - o Resize file system:
    - Ext4: sudo resize2fs /dev/vg_name/lv_name.
    - XFS: sudo xfs_growfs /dev/vg_name/lv_name.

By following this guide, you will gain confidence in managing Linux file systems, ensuring efficient storage utilization and system reliability.

Chapter 4: User and Group Management

Chapter Overview

This chapter provides an in-depth guide to managing users and groups in Linux. It covers the roles and characteristics of users and groups, creating and modifying accounts, setting permissions, and addressing common issues. Detailed examples and practical tips are included to help you master these essential administrative tasks.

The Role of User and Group Management

User and group management is crucial for:

- Controlling access to system resources.
- Assigning permissions to individuals or groups.
- Maintaining system security and stability.

Key Characteristics of Linux User Systems

- **What is a User in Linux?**
    - A user is an account that interacts with the system, each identified by a unique UID (User ID).
- **Types of Users**
    - **Root User**: Superuser with full control over the system.
    - **Standard Users**: Regular accounts for day-to-day tasks with limited permissions.
    - **System Users**: Accounts for system processes and services.
- **System Users vs. Standard Users**
    - System users typically do not have home directories and are not for direct login.
    - Standard users have home directories and are meant for human interaction.

Managing User Accounts

Task	Command Example	Description
Add a user	sudo adduser alice	Interactive method to create a user.
Modify a user	sudo usermod -aG sudo alice	Adds Alice to the sudo group.
Delete a user	sudo userdel -r alice	Removes Alice and her home directory.

Note: Always verify user actions with cat /etc/passwd after modifications.

Warning: Deleting a user without the -r option leaves their home directory intact, which could lead to security risks.

Configuring Password Policies

Policy	Command Example	Description
Password Expiry	sudo chage -M 90 alice	Sets Alice's password to expire in 90 days.
Minimum Password Length	Edit /etc/security/pwquality.conf	Defines minimum password length.
Complexity Requirements	Edit /etc/security/pwquality.conf	Enforces rules for special characters and digits.

Note: Strong password policies reduce unauthorized access risks.

Warning: Misconfigured policies can inadvertently lock users out of their accounts.

Group Management
What is a Group in Linux?

    o   A group is a collection of users with shared permissions.

Task	Command Example	Description
Add a group	sudo groupadd developers	Creates a group named 'developers'.
Remove a	sudo groupdel	Deletes the 'developers' group.

Task	Command Example	Description
group	developers	
Add a user to a group	sudo usermod -aG developers alice	Adds Alice to the 'developers' group.
Change primary group	sudo usermod -g developers alice	Changes Alice's primary group to 'developers'.

Note: Groups simplify permissions management for shared resources.

Warning: Ensure no files are owned by a group before deleting it to avoid access issues.

File Permissions and Ownership

Task	Command Example	Description
Change permissions	chmod 755 file.sh	Grants full permissions to owner, read/execute to others.
Change file ownership	sudo chown alice:developers file.sh	Changes owner to Alice and group to 'developers'.
Change group ownership	sudo chgrp developers file.sh	Changes group ownership to 'developers'.

Note: Always verify file permissions with ls -l before and after changes.

Warning: Avoid overly permissive settings (e.g., chmod 777), which can lead to security vulnerabilities.

Real-Life Examples

Scenario 1: Managing a Development Team

- **Problem**: A development team needs shared access to project files.
- **Solution**:
    1. Create a group: sudo groupadd devteam.
    2. Add users to the group: sudo usermod -aG devteam alice bob.
    3. Change group ownership: sudo chgrp -R devteam /projects.

4. Set permissions: sudo chmod -R 770 /projects.

Scenario 2: Recovering From Permission Errors
- **Problem**: Incorrect chmod caused access issues.
- **Solution**:
    1. Identify affected files: find /path/to/files -perm 777.
    2. Reset permissions: sudo chmod -R 750 /path/to/files.

Common Problems and Solutions
Problem: Locked Out Due to Password Policy
- **Cause**: Misconfigured complexity rules.
- **Solution**:
    o Boot into single-user mode.
    o Edit /etc/security/pwquality.conf to reduce complexity.
    o Reset the password with passwd username.

Problem: Group Membership Changes Not Effective Immediately
- **Cause**: Active session not refreshed.
- **Solution**:
    o Log out and log back in, or use newgrp groupname.

Best Practices
1. **Regular Audits**:
    o Review user accounts: cat /etc/passwd.
    o Remove unused accounts promptly.
2. **Use Access Control Lists (ACLs)**:
    o Enable ACLs: sudo mount -o remount,acl /filesystem.
    o Set specific permissions: setfacl -m u:username:rw file.
3. **Documentation**:
    o Maintain records of user and group changes for accountability.
    o Use descriptive names for easier management.
4. **Backups Before Changes**:
    o Backup critical files like /etc/passwd and /etc/group before modifications.

By mastering user and group management, you can secure your Linux environment, streamline administrative tasks, and ensure efficient resource control. This chapter equips you with the tools and knowledge to handle these tasks confidently.

Chapter 5: Software Management

Chapter Overview

This chapter provides a comprehensive guide to managing software in Linux. It explains the role of package managers, key concepts, step-by-step installation and update processes, repository management, troubleshooting, and best practices. Detailed examples and troubleshooting tips are included to ensure mastery of software management tasks.

The Role of Software Management

Software management is essential for:

- Installing and maintaining critical applications.
- Keeping the system secure and up-to-date.
- Managing repositories and resolving dependencies efficiently.

Key Characteristics of Linux Package Managers

Linux package managers simplify software management by automating installation, updates, and dependency resolution.

- **What is a Package Manager?**
  - A tool that automates software installation, updates, and removal.
  - Examples include APT, YUM, DNF, and Zypper.
- **Types of Package Managers**
  - **APT**: Widely used in Debian-based systems like Ubuntu.
  - **YUM/DNF**: Common in RHEL-based systems like CentOS and Fedora.
  - **Zypper**: Efficient for OpenSUSE systems.

Package Manager	Key Features	Example Commands
APT	Simple to use, wide adoption in Debian systems.	sudo apt install package_name
YUM/DNF	Robust dependency handling for RHEL/CentOS.	sudo yum install package_name

Package Manager	Key Features	Example Commands
Zypper	Fast and efficient for OpenSUSE.	sudo zypper install package_name

Note: Always use the package manager recommended for your distribution.

Warning: Mixing package managers (e.g., using APT and Snap for similar tasks) can lead to software conflicts.

Installing and Updating Software
Installing Software with APT

Task	Command Example	Description
Search for a package	sudo apt search package_name	Finds packages matching the name.
Install a package	sudo apt install package_name	Installs a single package.
Install multiple packages	sudo apt install package1 package2	Installs multiple packages simultaneously.

Updating Software with APT

Task	Command Example	Description
Update package list	sudo apt update	Refreshes the package database
Upgrade installed packages	sudo apt upgrade	Updates all installed packages
Full system upgrade	sudo apt full-upgrade	Upgrades packages with dependency changes.

Note: Frequent updates enhance system security and compatibilit

Warning: Backup critical data before performing system upgrade

Using YUM and DNF for CentOS/RHEL Systems

Task	Command Example	Description
Install a package	sudo yum install package_name	Installs a pac

Task	Command Example	Description
Remove a package	sudo yum remove package_name	Removes a package.
Update all packages	sudo yum update	Updates all installed packages.

Working with Zypper for OpenSUSE

Task	Command Example	Description
Install a package	sudo zypper install package_name	Installs a package.
Remove a package	sudo zypper remove package_name	Removes a package.
Update all packages	sudo zypper update	Updates all installed packages.

Managing Software Repositories

- **What is a Software Repository?**
  - A repository is a centralized storage location for software packages.
  - It ensures access to precompiled and verified software.

Command Example	Description
sudo add-apt-repository ppa:repo_name	Adds a PPA repository for APT.
do add-apt-repository -r repo_name	Removes a PPA repository.
update	Refreshes the repository database.

m trusted sources to minimize security

ositories can cause dependency

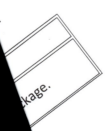

kage.

- **What are Snap and Flatpak?**
  - Universal package managers compatible across Linux distributions.

Tool	Command Example	Description
Snap	sudo snap install package_name	Installs a snap package.
Flatpak	flatpak install repo_name package_name	Installs a flatpak package.

Note: Snap and Flatpak simplify cross-distro software deployment by bundling dependencies.

Warning: Universal packages may consume more disk space compared to traditional package managers.

Troubleshooting Software Management Issues
Resolving Broken Dependencies
- **Problem**: Package installation fails due to dependency issues.
- **Solution**:
  1. For APT: sudo apt --fix-broken install.
  2. For YUM: sudo yum check-update to identify conflicts.

Clearing Cache and Rebuilding Package Databases
- **Problem**: Package manager errors due to corrupt cache.
- **Solution**:
  1. Clear APT cache: sudo apt clean.
  2. Rebuild the database: sudo apt update.

Note: Regular cache maintenance prevents storage issues and improves system performance.

Real-Life Examples
Scenario 1: Installing a LAMP Stack on Ubuntu
- **Problem**: You need to set up a web server with Apache, MySQL, and PHP.
- **Solution**:
  1. Update package lists: sudo apt update.
  2. Install Apache: sudo apt install apache2.
  3. Install MySQL: sudo apt install mysql-server.
  4. Install PHP: sudo apt install php libapache2-mod-php.
  5. Test the setup: Create a PHP file in /var/www/html and

access it via your browser.

Scenario 2: Resolving Dependency Issues on CentOS

- **Problem**: Installing software fails due to missing dependencies.
- **Solution**:
    1. Clear metadata: sudo yum clean metadata.
    2. Install the epel-release repository for additional packages: sudo yum install epel-release.
    3. Retry installation: sudo yum install package_name.

Common Errors and Solutions

Problem: "GPG Key Error" When Adding a Repository

- **Cause**: The repository's GPG key is not installed.
- **Solution**:
    1. Download the GPG key: wget -qO - https://repo_url/gpg.key | sudo apt-key add -.
    2. Update package lists: sudo apt update.

Problem: Conflicting Snap and APT Packages

- **Cause**: The same software is installed via Snap and APT, causing conflicts.
- **Solution**:
    1. Identify the conflicting package: snap list and apt list -- installed.
    2. Remove the unnecessary version: sudo snap remove package_name or sudo apt remove package_name.

Problem: Slow Package Updates on YUM

- **Cause**: Metadata cache is outdated or network mirrors are slow.
- **Solution**:
    1. Clear metadata: sudo yum clean all.
    2. Use a faster mirror: Edit /etc/yum.repos.d/repo_name.repo to prioritize a faster mirror.

Best Practices

1. **Schedule Regular Updates**:
    - Automate updates using cron or systemd timers.
2. **Backup Configurations**:

o   Backup key configuration files before system changes.

3. **Use Trusted Sources**:
    o   Avoid adding repositories from unverified sources to maintain system integrity.

4. **Monitor Logs**:
    o   Analyze logs in /var/log/apt/ or equivalent directories to diagnose errors.

5. **Minimize Redundancy**:
    o   Remove unused packages with sudo apt autoremove to save disk space.

By mastering software management, you ensure a stable, secure, and efficient Linux environment. This chapter equips you with the tools and knowledge to confidently handle software installations, updates, and troubleshooting across multiple distributions.

Chapter 6: Process and Service Management

Chapter Overview

This chapter focuses on managing processes and services in Linux. It introduces tools and techniques for monitoring, controlling, and optimizing system processes and services. You'll learn how to use commands like ps, top, and systemctl, as well as schedule tasks with cron and at. Troubleshooting tips and real-world examples are included to strengthen your understanding.

The Role of Process and Service Management

Process and service management is critical for:

*   Monitoring and optimizing system performance.
*   Managing active services for system stability.
*   Diagnosing and resolving system issues.
*   Ensuring system resources are allocated efficiently.

Key Characteristics of Linux Process Tools

Linux provides robust tools for process management, offering detailed insights into running tasks.

What is a Process in Linux?

- A process is an instance of a running program, identified by a unique Process ID (PID).
- Processes can be foreground (interactive) or background (non-interactive).

Foreground vs. Background Processes

- **Foreground**: Processes directly interact with the terminal, e.g., nano file.txt.
- **Background**: Processes run independently, often started with & or nohup. Examples include ./script.sh &.

Tool	Purpose	Example Command
ps	Lists running processes.	ps aux
top	Provides real-time process monitoring.	top
htop	Interactive process viewer with UI.	htop

Note: Use man to explore detailed documentation for these tools.

Warning: Misuse of commands like kill can terminate critical processes.

Understanding Linux Processes

Viewing Processes: ps Command Basics

Task	Command Example	Description
List all processes	ps aux	Displays all running processes.
Filter by user	ps -u username	Shows processes for a specific user.
Search for a process	`ps aux	grep process_name`

Interactive Monitoring with top and htop

- **top**:
  - Displays real-time system stats, including CPU and memory usage.
  - Use k within top to kill a process.

- **htop**:
  - Easier to navigate with arrow keys and function keys.
  - Use F9 to kill processes.
  - Allows filtering by resource usage.

Killing Processes Safely
- Use kill to terminate a process by PID.
  - Command: kill PID
  - Example: kill 1234
- Use killall to terminate processes by name.
  - Command: killall process_name
  - Example: killall firefox
- Use pkill for partial name matching.
  - Command: pkill -f partial_name

Note: Always identify critical processes before termination.

Warning: Killing system processes can destabilize the system. Check with ps before executing kill.

Managing Services with Systemd
Systemd is a modern service manager used in most Linux distrisutions for managing system and application services.

- **Introduction to Systemd**
  - Systemd is a suite of tools and libraries for managing system processes.
  - Key components include systemctl for service management and journalctl for log analysis.

Starting and Stopping Services

Task	Command Example	Description
Start a service	sudo systemctl start service_name	Starts the specified service.
Stop a service	sudo systemctl stop service_name	Stops the specified service.

Checking the Status of a Service

Task	Command Example	Description
Check service	sudo systemctl status	Shows whether a service

Task	Command Example	Description
status	service_name	is running.
View active services	sudo systemctl list-units --type=service	Lists all active services.

Enabling and Disabling Services at Boot

Task	Command Example	Description
Enable a service	sudo systemctl enable service_name	Starts the service at boot.
Disable a service	sudo systemctl disable service_name	Prevents the service from starting at boot.

Note: Enabled services automatically start during boot-up.

Warning: Disabling essential services may prevent the system from functioning correctly. Verify dependencies with systemctl list-dependencies.

Debugging Failing Services

- Use journalctl to view service logs:
  - Command: sudo journalctl -u service_name
  - Example: sudo journalctl -u apache2
- Restart the service after troubleshooting:
  - Command: sudo systemctl restart service_name

Note: Combine journalctl with grep for targeted log analysis.

Scheduling Processes and Jobs
Understanding Cron Jobs

- Cron automates repetitive tasks such as backups and log cleanups.

Task	Command Example	Description
List cron jobs	crontab -l	Displays scheduled tasks for the user.
Edit cron jobs	crontab -e	Opens the cron table for editing.

Example Cron Entry:

- Schedule a daily backup:
  - 0 2 * * * tar -czf /backup/$(date +\%F).tar.gz /data
  - Runs at 2 AM daily.

One-Time Scheduling with at Command

- Schedule a one-time task with at.
    - Command: echo "command" | at time
    - Example: echo "shutdown now" | at 10:00 AM

Note: Use atq to view pending jobs and atrm to remove them.

Warning: Incorrect cron syntax can lead to unintended task scheduling.

Troubleshooting Common Process Issues
Identifying High CPU/Memory Usage
- Use top or htop to locate resource-intensive processes.
- Monitor logs in /var/log/syslog for anomalies.

Restarting Stuck Processes
- Use systemctl restart for services:
    - Command: sudo systemctl restart service_name
    - Example: sudo systemctl restart nginx

Note: Monitor logs for recurring issues and investigate root causes.

Warning: Repeatedly restarting processes without resolving issues may mask underlying problems.

Real-Life Examples
Scenario 1: Restarting a Web Server
- **Problem**: Your Apache server stops responding.
- **Solution**:
    1. Check the service status: sudo systemctl status apache2.
    2. Restart the service: sudo systemctl restart apache2.
    3. View logs: sudo journalctl -u apache2 for errors.

Scenario 2: Scheduling Backups with Cron
- **Problem**: Automate daily backups at midnight.
- **Solution**:
    1. Open the cron table: crontab -e.
    2. Add the job: 0 0 * * * tar -czf /backup/$(date +\%F).tar.gz /data.

Common Errors and Solutions
Problem: Service Fails to Start
- **Cause**: Configuration errors or missing dependencies.
- **Solution**:

1. Check logs: sudo journalctl -u service_name.
2. Verify configuration files for syntax errors.

Problem: Cron Job Not Executing

- **Cause**: Incorrect syntax or missing cron daemon.
- **Solution**:
    1. Verify syntax: Ensure correct format in crontab -e.
    2. Check if the cron daemon is running: sudo systemctl status cron.

Best Practices

1. **Monitor Critical Services**:
    o Use tools like systemd or Nagios for proactive monitoring.
2. **Document Custom Jobs**:
    o Maintain records of scheduled tasks and custom configurations.
3. **Test Before Deployment**:
    o Validate cron jobs and at commands in a test environment.
4. **Backup Configurations**:
    o Backup critical service configuration files before modifications.
5. **Use Automation Wisely**:
    o Avoid overloading cron with tasks that can be batched or consolidated.

By mastering process and service management, you ensure a stable and efficient Linux system. This chapter equips you with tools and techniques to monitor, control, and optimize processes and services effectively.

Chapter 7: Networking and Remote Access

Chapter Overview

This chapter explores networking and remote access in Linux. It covers basic network concepts, configuring network interfaces, managing hostnames and DNS settings, and enabling secure remote access using

SSH. Practical tools for network troubleshooting and step-by-step examples provide a comprehensive understanding of these essential skills.

.

The Role of Networking in Linux

Networking enables communication between devices, applications, and servers. In Linux, effective network management is critical for:

- Ensuring connectivity and system reliability.
- Configuring and troubleshooting network interfaces.
- Securely accessing remote systems.
- Managing resource sharing and collaboration within networks.

Key Characteristics of Remote Access Tools

Remote access tools like SSH are crucial for:

- Secure communication with remote servers.
- Managing systems without physical access.
- Automating administrative tasks through scripting.
- Transferring files securely using protocols like SFTP and SCP.

Understanding Network Basics
What is a Network Interface?

- A network interface connects a device to a network, allowing it to send and receive data.
- Examples include:
    - **Ethernet interfaces**: eth0, ens33.
    - **Wireless interfaces**: wlan0, wlp2s0.
    - **Loopback interface**: lo (used for local communication).

Types of Networks

- **LAN (Local Area Network)**: Covers a small geographical area, such as a home or office.
- **WAN (Wide Area Network)**: Connects LANs over a large area, such as the internet.
- **VPN (Virtual Private Network)**: Creates secure connections to private networks over public networks.

Note: Use ip a to list all network interfaces on your system.

Configuring Network Interfaces
What is an IP Address?

- An IP address uniquely identifies a device on a network.
- Types of IP addresses:

- o **IPv4**: Format: 192.168.1.1.
- o **IPv6**: Format: 2001:0db8:85a3::8a2e:0370:7334.

Static vs. Dynamic IPs

IP Type	Use Case	Example
Static	Servers, printers, or critical systems.	192.168.1.100/24
Dynamic	Personal devices, guest systems.	Assigned via DHCP.

Using nmcli for Configuration

- • **View current network configurations**:
  - o Command: nmcli dev show
- • **Assign a static IP**:
  - o Command: nmcli con mod "connection_name" ipv4.addresses "192.168.1.100/24" ipv4.gateway "192.168.1.1" ipv4.method manual
  - o Restart the connection: nmcli con up "connection_name"

Warning: Incorrect IP configurations can disconnect your system from the network. Verify settings with ip a.

Hostnames and DNS Settings

What is a Hostname?

- • A hostname identifies a device on a network for easier recognition.
- • View the current hostname:
  - o Command: hostnamectl
- • Change the hostname:
  - o Command: sudo hostnamectl set-hostname new_hostname

Editing /etc/hosts for Name Resolution

- • **Purpose**: Maps hostnames to IP addresses for local resolution.
- • Example entry:
  - o 127.0.0.1 localhost
  - o 192.168.1.100 server.local

Understanding /etc/resolv.conf for DNS

- • **Purpose**: Defines DNS servers for resolving domain names.
- • Example entry:
  - o nameserver 8.8.8.8

      o   nameserver 8.8.4.4

Configuring Persistent DNS Settings

- Use NetworkManager to ensure settings persist:
  - Command: nmcli con mod "connection_name" ipv4.dns "8.8.8.8 8.8.4.4"
  - Restart the connection: nmcli con up "connection_name"

Note: Verify DNS changes with ping google.com or nslookup google.com.

Secure Remote Access with SSH

Introduction to SSH: Why Use It?

- Secure Shell (SSH) provides encrypted communication for remote management.
- Commonly used for:
  - Remote server access.
  - File transfers using scp or rsync.
  - Port forwarding and tunneling.

Installing and Configuring an SSH Server

- **Install OpenSSH Server**:
  - Command: sudo apt install openssh-server
- **Check SSH service status**:
  - Command: sudo systemctl status ssh

Key-Based Authentication Setup

Task	Command Example	Description
Generate SSH keys	ssh-keygen -t rsa -b 4096	Creates public/private key pair.
Copy public key to remote server	ssh-copy-id user@remote_server	Enables key-based authentication.

Note: Key-based authentication is more secure than passwords.

Warning: After setting up keys, disable password authentication in /etc/ssh/sshd_config for enhanced security.

Network Troubleshooting Tools

What is ping and When to Use It

- **Purpose**: Tests connectivity to a specific host.
- Example:

       o   Command: ping google.com

Diagnosing Routes with traceroute

- **Purpose**: Traces the path packets take to a destination.
- Example:
  - o   Command: traceroute google.com

Analyzing Connections with netstat and ss

- **netstat**: Displays active connections and listening ports.
  - o   Example: netstat -tuln
- **ss**: A modern alternative to netstat with faster performance.
  - o   Example: ss -tuln

Note: Use sudo for more detailed output with these tools.

Real-Life Examples

Scenario 1: Setting Up a Static IP for a Server

- **Problem**: A server needs a permanent IP for consistent access.
- **Solution**:
  1. Use nmcli to configure a static IP.
  2. Verify the settings with ip a.
  3. Test connectivity with ping.

Scenario 2: Troubleshooting SSH Connectivity

- **Problem**: Unable to SSH into a server.
- **Solution**:
  1. Check if the server is reachable:
     - Command: ping server_ip
  2. Verify the SSH service status:
     - Command: sudo systemctl status ssh
  3. Examine firewall settings:
     - Command: sudo ufw status

Common Errors and Solutions

Problem: DNS Resolution Fails

- **Cause**: Incorrect or missing DNS configuration.
- **Solution**:
  1. Verify /etc/resolv.conf for valid nameserver entries.
  2. Restart the network connection: nmcli con up "connection_name".

Problem: SSH Connection Refused
- **Cause**: SSH service not running or firewall blocking the port.
- **Solution**:
    1. Start the SSH service: sudo systemctl start ssh.
    2. Allow SSH through the firewall: sudo ufw allow ssh.

Best Practices
1. **Secure Remote Access**:
    - o Use key-based authentication for SSH.
    - o Disable root login via SSH for added security.
2. **Regularly Update Network Configurations**:
    - o Keep DNS and IP settings up-to-date for reliability.
3. **Monitor Network Performance**:
    - o Use tools like ping, traceroute, and ss to proactively identify issues.
4. **Document Changes**:
    - o Maintain a log of network and SSH configurations for future reference.

By mastering networking and remote access, you ensure efficient communication and secure management of Linux systems. This chapter equips you with the skills to configure networks, troubleshoot issues, and establish reliable remote connections.

Chapter 8: Storage and Disk Management

Chapter Overview

This chapter delves into managing storage and disks in Linux. It covers essential concepts such as disk and storage basics, partitioning, file system management, Logical Volume Manager (LVM), and monitoring disk usage. Real-world examples, best practices, and troubleshooting techniques provide a comprehensive guide to mastering these critical tasks.

The Role of Storage Management

Storage management is vital for:
- Organizing and storing data efficiently.
- Ensuring data availability and reliability.
- Optimizing storage resources for performance.
- Preparing systems for scalability and future storage needs.

Key Characteristics of Disk Management Tools

Linux provides various tools for managing disks and storage:
- **fdisk**: A basic tool for partitioning disks.
- **parted**: Advanced partitioning tool with support for modern partition schemes.
- **mkfs**: Formats partitions with a specific file system.
- **lsblk**: Displays information about block devices.
- **du/df**: Monitors disk usage and available space.
- **lsattr/chattr**: Manage file attributes for added control.

Note: Choose tools based on your system's requirements and complexity.

Understanding Disk and Storage Basics
What is Disk Storage?
- Disk storage is a medium for saving data persistently.
- Types include:
    - **HDDs (Hard Disk Drives)**: Cost-effective with large capacity but slower speeds.
    - **SSDs (Solid State Drives)**: Faster and more durable but more expensive.
    - **Network Storage**: Centralized storage accessible over a

network (e.g., NFS, iSCSI).

Types of Storage Devices

Type	Advantages	Disadvantages
HDD	Cost-effective, high capacity	Slower performance, mechanical parts.
SSD	High speed, no moving parts	Expensive per GB.
Network Storage	Centralized access, scalable	Requires network setup.

Additional Concepts

- **RAID (Redundant Array of Independent Disks)**:
  - Combines multiple disks for redundancy or performance.
  - Common levels: RAID 0, 1, 5, and 10.
- **File System Journaling**:
  - Protects against corruption during unexpected shutdowns.
  - Supported by ext4, xfs, and others.

Managing Partitions and File Systems

What is a Partition?

- A partition divides a disk into logical sections for better organization.
- Each partition can have its own file system and use case (e.g., /, /home, /var).

Creating Partitions with fdisk

1. Launch fdisk:
   - Command: sudo fdisk /dev/sdX
2. Create a new partition:
   - Command: n
3. Save changes:
   - Command: w

Using parted for Advanced Partitioning

- **View existing partitions**:
  - Command: sudo parted /dev/sdX print
- **Create a new partition**:

- Command: sudo parted /dev/sdX mkpart primary ext4 1MiB 100GiB

Formatting Partitions with mkfs
- Format a partition with a file system:
  - Command: sudo mkfs.ext4 /dev/sdX1
- Supported file systems:
  - ext4, xfs, vfat, etc.

Labeling Partitions
- Use e2label for ext4 partitions:
  - Command: sudo e2label /dev/sdX1 data_partition

Note: Use mkfs carefully as it erases existing data on the partition.

Mounting and Unmounting File Systems
What Does Mounting Mean?
- Mounting makes a partition accessible to the system by attaching it to a directory.

Temporary vs. Permanent Mounts

Type	Use Case	Example Command
Temporary	Mounts for immediate, short-term use.	sudo mount /dev/sdX1 /mnt/data
Permanent	Automatically mounts at boot.	Configure in /etc/fstab.

Configuring /etc/fstab for Persistent Mounts
- Example entry:
  - /dev/sdX1 /mnt/data ext4 defaults 0 2

Warning: Errors in /etc/fstab can prevent the system from booting. Test entries with sudo mount -a.

Checking Mount Options
- Verify active mount options with mount:
  - Command: mount | grep /mnt/data

Logical Volume Manager (LVM)
Introduction to LVM: Benefits and Use Cases
- LVM abstracts physical storage into logical volumes for flexibility.
- Benefits include:
  - Dynamic resizing of storage.

- o Combining multiple disks into a single volume group.
- o Snapshots for backups and testing.

Steps to Create and Manage Logical Volumes
1. Create a physical volume:
   - o Command: sudo pvcreate /dev/sdX
2. Create a volume group:
   - o Command: sudo vgcreate vg_name /dev/sdX
3. Create a logical volume:
   - o Command: sudo lvcreate -L 10G -n lv_name vg_name

Extending and Resizing LVM Partitions
- Extend a logical volume:
  - o Command: sudo lvextend -L +5G /dev/vg_name/lv_name
- Resize the file system:
  - o Command (ext4): sudo resize2fs /dev/vg_name/lv_name

Snapshots with LVM
- Create a snapshot:
  - o Command: sudo lvcreate --size 1G --snapshot --name snap_name /dev/vg_name/lv_name

Note: Backup data before resizing partitions to prevent data loss.

Disk Quotas and Usage Monitoring
What is a Disk Quota?
- Disk quotas limit the amount of storage a user or group can consume.

Setting Up and Managing Quotas
1. Enable quotas in /etc/fstab:
   - o Example: /dev/sdX1 /home ext4 defaults,usrquota,grpquota 0 2
2. Remount the file system:
   - o Command: sudo mount -o remount /home
3. Initialize quota tracking:
   - o Command: sudo quotacheck -cug /home
4. Set user quota:
   - o Command: sudo setquota -u username 5000 5500 0 0 /home

Monitoring Disk Usage with du and df

Tool	Purpose	Example Command
du	Shows disk usage of directories and files.	du -sh /home/username
df	Displays available and used disk space.	df -h

Real-Life Examples
Scenario 1: Resizing a Partition on a Live System
- **Problem**: The /home partition is running out of space.
- **Solution**:
    1. Unmount the partition:
        - Command: sudo umount /home
    2. Resize the partition with parted:
        - Command: sudo parted /dev/sdX resizepart 2 100G
    3. Resize the file system:
        - Command: sudo resize2fs /dev/sdX2
    4. Remount the partition:
        - Command: sudo mount /home

Scenario 2: Setting Up Shared Storage with NFS
- **Problem**: Multiple systems need access to a shared storage location.
- **Solution**:
    1. Install NFS server:
        - Command: sudo apt install nfs-kernel-server
    2. Configure export directory in /etc/exports:
        - Example: /shared *(rw,sync,no_root_squash)
    3. Start the NFS service:
        - Command: sudo systemctl start nfs-server
    4. Mount the NFS share on clients:
        - Command: sudo mount server_ip:/shared /mnt/shared

Common Errors and Solutions
Problem: "Disk Full" on Critical Partition
- **Cause**: Excessive files or logs occupying space.

- **Solution**:
    1. Identify large directories:
        - Command: sudo du -sh /var/*
    2. Remove unnecessary files or logs:
        - Command: sudo rm /var/log/old_logs.log
    3. Consider adding space using LVM.

Problem: Failed LVM Volume
- **Cause**: Physical volume failure or corruption.
- **Solution**:
    1. Check volume group status:
        - Command: sudo vgdisplay
    2. Remove the faulty disk:
        - Command: sudo vgreduce vg_name /dev/sdX
    3. Replace the disk and add it back:
        - Command: sudo vgextend vg_name /dev/sdY

Problem: Filesystem Corruption
- **Cause**: Improper shutdown or disk failure.
- **Solution**:
    1. Unmount the affected partition:
        - Command: sudo umount /dev/sdX1
    2. Run fsck to repair:
        - Command: sudo fsck /dev/sdX1

Warning: Use fsck with caution on mounted partitions to avoid data corruption.

Best Practices
1. **Regular Backups**:
    - Use tools like rsync or tar for periodic backups.
    - Automate backups with cron or systemd timers.
2. **Monitor Storage Health**:
    - Use smartctl to monitor disk health and anticipate failures.
    - Example: sudo smartctl -a /dev/sdX
3. **Document Storage Configurations**:
    - Maintain a record of partition layouts, LVM setups, and /etc/fstab entries.

4. **Plan for Scalability**:
   - Use LVM or network storage solutions to accommodate future growth.
5. **Implement RAID for Redundancy**:
   - Use RAID configurations like RAID 1 (mirroring) or RAID 5 (striping with parity) to protect critical data.
6. **Check Inode Usage**:
   - Prevent "no space left on device" errors by monitoring inodes with df -i.
7. **Test Changes in a Sandbox Environment**:
   - Before deploying major storage changes, test in a virtual or isolated environment to minimize risks.

By mastering storage and disk management, you can efficiently organize and maintain data, ensure system reliability, and optimize performance. This chapter equips you with the skills to handle storage-related tasks confidently in any Linux environment.

Chapter 9: System Monitoring and Performance Tuning

Chapter Overview

This chapter explores the tools and techniques for monitoring and optimizing system performance in Linux. You'll learn about resource monitoring, managing system logs, identifying bottlenecks, and tuning the CPU, memory, and disk I/O for optimal performance. Practical examples and best practices are included to reinforce your understanding.

Note

- System monitoring tools can generate high resource usage during execution, especially on resource-constrained systems. Use them judiciously during peak hours.

Warning

- Modifying critical system parameters without understanding their impact can destabilize your system. Always test changes in a controlled environment.

The Role of System Monitoring

System monitoring is essential for:

- Maintaining system health and reliability.
- Diagnosing performance issues.
- Proactively addressing potential system failures.
- Ensuring efficient resource utilization.

Key Characteristics of Performance Optimization

Performance optimization involves:

- Identifying and addressing bottlenecks.
- Ensuring balanced resource usage across CPU, memory, and storage.
- Implementing tools to automate performance tracking and alerts.

Monitoring CPU, Memory, and Disk Usage

What is System Monitoring?

- System monitoring tracks resource usage to provide insights into system health and performance.

- Key metrics include:
    - **CPU usage**: Tracks processor load.
    - **Memory usage**: Measures active and available memory.
    - **Disk I/O**: Monitors read/write operations on storage.

Tools for Monitoring Resources

Tool	Purpose	Example Command
top	Displays real-time CPU, memory, and process usage.	top
htop	Interactive monitoring with a user-friendly interface.	htop
iostat	Provides detailed disk performance metrics.	iostat -x 1
free	Displays memory usage statistics.	free -h
vmstat	Provides detailed system performance stats.	vmstat 5

Using top for Process Monitoring

- **Purpose**: Real-time monitoring of system processes.
- **Features**:
    - CPU and memory usage per process.
    - Load averages over time.
- **Example Commands**:
    - Launch top: top
    - Sort by memory usage: Press M
    - Kill a process: Press k and enter the PID.

Understanding htop for Interactive Monitoring

- **Purpose**: Interactive and visually rich monitoring tool.
- **Features**:
    - Navigate processes using arrow keys.
    - Highlight resource-intensive processes.
- **Example Commands**:
    - Launch htop: htop
    - Search for a process: Press / and type the name.

o   Kill a process: Select it and press F9.

Analyzing Disk Performance with iostat
- **Purpose**: Monitors disk I/O performance.
- **Example Command**:
    o   iostat -x 1: Displays extended stats updated every second.
- **Metrics Explained**:
    o   **%util**: Disk utilization percentage.
    o   **await**: Average time for I/O requests.

Monitoring Memory Usage with free
- **Purpose**: Tracks memory consumption and availability.
- **Example Command**:
    o   free -h: Displays memory usage in a human-readable format.
- **Key Metrics**:
    o   **Used memory**: Currently in use.
    o   **Available memory**: Free for new processes.

Using vmstat for Detailed System Statistics
- **Purpose**: Provides comprehensive stats on processes, memory, and I/O.
- **Example Command**:
    o   vmstat 5: Updates metrics every 5 seconds.
- **Metrics Explained**:
    o   **r**: Processes waiting for CPU.
    o   **b**: Processes blocked for I/O.
    o   **si/so**: Swap-in and swap-out rates.

Managing System Logs
What are System Logs?
- Logs provide a record of system events and errors.
- Common types include:
    o   **Kernel logs**: Track kernel events.
    o   **Application logs**: Record software-specific activity.

Common Log Locations: /var/log Overview

- Key directories:
  - /var/log/syslog or /var/log/messages: General system logs.
  - /var/log/auth.log: Authentication logs.
  - /var/log/dmesg: Boot and kernel logs.

Viewing Logs with journalctl

- **Purpose**: Access logs managed by systemd.
- **Example Commands**:
  - View all logs: sudo journalctl
  - Filter by service: sudo journalctl -u service_name

Searching and Filtering Logs for Errors

- Use grep to filter logs for errors:
  - Example: grep "error" /var/log/syslog

Rotating Logs to Save Space

- **Purpose**: Prevent logs from consuming excessive disk space.
- **Tool**: logrotate
- **Example**:
  - Configure rotation in /etc/logrotate.conf.

Real-Life Scenarios

Scenario 1: Resolving High CPU Usage

- **Problem**: A process consumes 100% CPU, slowing down the system.
- **Solution**:
  1. Identify the process:
     - Command: top or htop
  2. Kill the process:
     - Command: sudo kill PID
  3. Investigate logs for root cause:
     - Example: Check /var/log/syslog.

Scenario 2: Troubleshooting Disk I/O Bottlenecks

- **Problem**: Applications slow due to high disk usage.
- **Solution**:
  1. Analyze disk I/O:
     - Command: iostat -x

2. Identify resource-heavy applications with iotop.
3. Optimize file system parameters or move to faster storage (e.g., SSD).

Scenario 3: Optimizing Memory Usage

- **Problem**: Swap space is overutilized, causing system lag.
- **Solution**:
  1. Increase swap space:
     - Command: sudo fallocate -l 2G /swapfile
  2. Monitor memory with free -h to ensure stability.

Common Errors and Solutions

Problem: Excessive Logs Consuming Disk Space

- **Cause**: Log rotation misconfiguration.
- **Solution**:
  1. Verify logrotate configuration:
     - Command: sudo cat /etc/logrotate.conf
  2. Manually rotate logs:
     - Command: sudo logrotate -f /etc/logrotate.conf

Problem: System Unresponsive Due to High Load

- **Cause**: Resource-intensive processes or hardware limits.
- **Solution**:
  1. Check system load:
     - Command: uptime
  2. Identify processes:
     - Command: top
  3. Reduce load by terminating unnecessary tasks.

Problem: Logs Missing in journalctl

- **Cause**: Journal logs storage limited by configuration.
- **Solution**:
  1. Increase journal storage:
     - Command: sudo nano /etc/systemd/journald.conf
     - Update: SystemMaxUse=500M
  2. Restart the service:
     - Command: sudo systemctl restart systemd-journald

Performance Optimization Techniques

Identifying System Bottlenecks

- Use monitoring tools to pinpoint:
    - High CPU usage.
    - Insufficient memory.
    - Slow disk performance.

Tuning CPU Performance

- Adjust CPU scheduling priorities:
    - Command: sudo renice -n priority_level -p PID
- Disable unnecessary services to free CPU cycles.

Optimizing Disk I/O

- Use faster file systems (e.g., xfs or ext4).
- Employ disk caching with hdparm.
    - Example: sudo hdparm -W1 /dev/sdX

Reducing Memory Pressure

- Increase swap space:
    - Create a swap file:
        - Command: sudo fallocate -l 2G /swapfile
        - Enable it: sudo swapon /swapfile
- Optimize applications to use memory efficiently.

Best Practices

1. **Automate Monitoring**:
    - Use tools like Prometheus or Nagios to set up alerts for resource thresholds.
2. **Log Retention Policies**:
    - Define log rotation and retention policies to manage disk usage effectively.
3. **Regular Maintenance**:
    - Schedule regular checks using cron or systemd timers for tools like fsck and smartctl.
4. **Document Changes**:
    - Maintain records of tuning adjustments for future audits and troubleshooting.
5. **Test in Sandbox Environments**:
    - Use virtual environments to test new configurations

before applying them to production.

6. **Optimize Applications**:
   o Work closely with developers to identify and address inefficiencies in software.
   o Utilize profiling tools like perf or strace to identify bottlenecks in applications.
   o Ensure applications use resources like CPU and memory efficiently by following best practices and regular code reviews.

Conclusion

By mastering system monitoring and performance tuning, administrators can ensure optimal performance, stability, and reliability in Linux environments. Utilizing the tools and techniques outlined in this chapter will empower you to proactively address issues and maintain a high-performing system.

Chapter 10: Backup and Recovery

Chapter Overview

This chapter focuses on the critical aspects of creating, managing, and restoring backups in Linux. You will learn about the importance of backup strategies, various backup tools, automating backups, troubleshooting issues, and methods for data recovery. Practical examples and best practices are included to help you develop reliable backup and recovery processes.

Note

- Always verify the integrity of your backups by performing periodic restore tests. This ensures data consistency and reliability.

Warning

- Storing backups on the same physical device as the original data can lead to total data loss in case of hardware failure. Use separate devices or locations for backups.

The Role of Backup Strategies

Backup strategies are essential for:

- Protecting data from loss due to hardware failures, accidental deletions, or cyberattacks.
- Ensuring business continuity by enabling quick data recovery.
- Supporting disaster recovery plans.

Key Characteristics of Backup Tools

Backup tools in Linux should:

- Support different types of backups (full, incremental, differen
- Be reliable and efficient in managing large data sets.
- Provide automation and scheduling capabilities.

Importance of Backup Strategies

What is a Backup and Why is it Necessary?

- A backup is a copy of data stored separately to preven case of failures.
- Backups are necessary to:
  - Restore systems quickly after a crash.

- o Retrieve accidentally deleted files.
- o Comply with data protection regulations.

Types of Backups

1. **Full Backup**:
   - o Copies all data.
   - o Pros: Comprehensive and easy to restore.
   - o Cons: Time-consuming and requires significant storage.

2. **Incremental Backup**:
   - o Copies only data changed since the last backup.
   - o Pros: Fast and uses less storage.
   - o Cons: Slower restoration as multiple backups must be combined.

3. **Differential Backup**:
   - o Copies data changed since the last full backup.
   - o Pros: Faster restoration than incremental backups.
   - o Cons: Larger storage requirements than incremental backups.

ıe	Storage Requirements	Speed (Backup)	Speed (Restore)
	High	Slow	Fast
ıtal	Low	Fast	Slow
	Medium	Medium	Medium

ıg Files Across Systems

ʰhronize files and directories between locations.

ʼansfer by copying only changed files.

SSH for secure backups.

e_directory/

kup_directory/

ʒ Files

ƈ and directories.

ıtial).

loss in

ıes into one.

- o Supports compression with gzip or bzip2.
- **Example Command**:
  - o Create a compressed archive: tar -cvzf backup.tar.gz /source_directory/

Using GUI-Based Backup Tools for Beginners
- Examples:
  - o **Timeshift**: Ideal for system snapshots.
  - o **Deja Dup**: User-friendly tool for regular backups.
- **Features**:
  - o Simple interfaces for scheduling and managing backups.
  - o Integration with cloud storage providers.

Automating Backups
What are Cron Jobs?
- Cron is a scheduling tool used to automate tasks in Linux.
- **Example Cron Entry**:
  - o 0 2 * * * rsync -avz /source_directory/ /backup_directory/
  - o Runs rsync every day at 2 AM.

Setting Up and Scheduling Backup Tasks with Cron
1. Edit the crontab file:
   - o Command: crontab -e
2. Add a backup schedule:
   - o Example: 0 3 * * 7 tar -cvzf /backup/weekly_backup.tar.gz /data_directory/

Testing Automated Backups for Reliability
- Verify cron jobs:
  - o Command: sudo systemctl status cron
- Test restore process:
  - o Extract and compare backed-up data.

Troubleshooting Backup and Recovery
Problem: Backup Fails Due to Insufficient Space
- **Cause**: The backup destination lacks free space.
- **Solution**:
  1. Check available space:
     - ▪ Command: df -h

2. Remove old or unnecessary backups to free space.
3. Use compression tools like gzip with tar to reduce backup size.

Problem: Automated Backup Fails to Execute

- **Cause**: Cron job misconfiguration or disabled cron service.
- **Solution**:
    1. Verify cron service status:
        - Command: sudo systemctl status cron
    2. Check the crontab file for syntax errors:
        - Command: crontab -l
    3. Test the backup script manually to ensure functionality.

Problem: Corrupted Backup Archive

- **Cause**: Errors during the backup creation process.
- **Solution**:
    1. Verify the archive:
        - Command: tar -tvf backup.tar.gz
    2. Recreate the backup and ensure no interruptions during the process.
    3. Use tools like md5sum to validate file integrity.

Data Recovery Methods

What is Data Recovery?

- Data recovery is the process of retrieving lost or corrupted data from storage devices.

Using testdisk for Partition Recovery

- **Purpose**: Recover lost partitions and make non-bootable disks bootable.
- **Steps**:
    1. Install testdisk:
        - Command: sudo apt install testdisk
    2. Run testdisk:
        - Command: sudo testdisk
    3. Follow prompts to scan and recover partitions.

Exploring Advanced Recovery Tools

- **photorec**:
    - Specializes in recovering lost files from storage devices.

- o   Command: sudo photorec
- **ddrescue**:
  - o   Recovers data from damaged disks.
  - o   Command: sudo ddrescue /dev/sdX /output.img /logfile

Best Practices

1. **Maintain Multiple Backup Copies**:
   - o   Follow the 3-2-1 rule: 3 copies of your data, 2 different storage mediums, 1 offsite.
2. **Encrypt Sensitive Backups**:
   - o   Use tools like gpg to encrypt backup archives.
   - o   Example: gpg -c backup.tar.gz
3. **Regularly Test Backups**:
   - o   Perform restoration tests to ensure data integrity.
4. **Automate Alerts**:
   - o   Set up email or SMS alerts for backup failures.
5. **Document Backup Policies**:
   - o   Clearly define schedules, tools, and procedures in an accessible document.
6. **Use Redundant Backup Locations**:
   - o   Store backups in geographically separate locations to mitigate regional risks.

Conclusion

Implementing robust backup and recovery strategies is essential for safeguarding your data and ensuring quick restoration in case of failures. By leveraging tools like rsync, tar, and testdisk, and adhering to best practices, you can build a reliable system that minimizes data loss and downtime.

Chapter 11: Security and Hardening

Chapter Overview

This chapter focuses on securing Linux systems by exploring essential hardening techniques and tools. It covers regular updates, firewall configuration, enhanced security with SELinux and AppArmor, and monitoring for breaches. Practical examples and actionable steps are included to help you strengthen your system's security.

The Role of Security in Linux

Security in Linux involves:

- Protecting systems from unauthorized access.
- Mitigating vulnerabilities with proactive measures.
- Monitoring and responding to potential threats.

Key Characteristics of Hardening Techniques

Hardening techniques enhance system security by:

- Reducing attack surfaces.
- Implementing access controls.
- Using tools for proactive monitoring and defense.

Keeping Your System Secure

Regular Updates and Patches

Task	Command Example	Description
Update package lists	sudo apt update	Ensures the latest package information.
Apply updates	sudo apt upgrade	Installs available updates.
Automate updates	Add to cron: 0 3 * * * apt update && apt upgrade -y	Schedules updates daily at 3 AM.

Why Updates Matter:

- Address known vulnerabilities.
- Improve software stability and compatibility.

Note: Always test critical updates in a staging environment before applying to production.

Warning: Delaying updates may expose the system to exploitable vulnerabilities.

Configuring Firewalls
What is a Firewall?

A firewall controls incoming and outgoing network traffic based on predefined security rules.

Basics of ufw (Uncomplicated Firewall)

Task	Command Example	Description
Enable the firewall	sudo ufw enable	Activates the firewall.
Disable the firewall	sudo ufw disable	Deactivates the firewall.
Allow SSH traffic	sudo ufw allow ssh	Permits SSH connections.
Deny a port	sudo ufw deny 8080	Blocks traffic on port 8080.

Creating Rules with ufw
- Allow HTTP and HTTPS:
    - sudo ufw allow 80 (HTTP)
    - sudo ufw allow 443 (HTTPS)
- View active rules:
    - sudo ufw status

Note: Use ufw status verbose for detailed output.

Introduction to iptables
- **Chains and Rules**:
    - Chains: Input, Output, Forward.
    - Rules: Define how packets are handled within chains.
- Example: Block all incoming traffic except SSH:
- sudo iptables -A INPUT -p tcp --dport 22 -j ACCEPT
- sudo iptables -A INPUT -j DROP

Warning: Misconfigured iptables rules can lock you out of the system.

Using SELinux and AppArmor
What is SELinux?

SELinux (Security-Enhanced Linux) enforces mandatory access controls to enhance system security.

Configuring SELinux Modes

Mode	Command Example	Description
Enforcing	sudo setenforce 1	Enforces all SELinux policies.
Permissive	sudo setenforce 0	Logs violations without enforcing policies.
Disabled	Modify /etc/selinux/config and reboot	Turns off SELinux completely.

What is AppArmor?

AppArmor restricts applications by defining profiles that limit their capabilities.

Setting Up Profiles in AppArmor

Task	Command Example	Description
List profiles	sudo aa-status	Displays loaded AppArmor profiles.
Enforce a profile	sudo aa-enforce /path/to/profile	Activates a profile in enforce mode.
Disable a profile	sudo aa-disable /path/to/profile	Deactivates a specific profile.

Note: Use aa-genprof to generate new profiles interactively.

Monitoring Security Breaches

What is Intrusion Detection?

Intrusion detection identifies unauthorized access or suspicious activities on a system.

Overview of Intrusion Detection Tools

- **AIDE** (Advanced Intrusion Detection Environment): Monitors file integrity.
- **OSSEC**: Provides real-time log analysis and intrusion detection.

Setting Up and Using AIDE

Task	Command Example	Description
Initialize the database	sudo aide --init	Creates a baseline database.

Task	Command Example	Description
Check for changes	sudo aide --check	Compares the current state to the baseline.
Update the database	sudo aide --update	Refreshes the baseline after authorized changes.

Monitoring Logs for Unusual Activity

Task	Command Example	Description
View authentication logs	sudo cat /var/log/auth.log	Checks login attempts and failures.
Search logs with grep	sudo grep "keyword" /var/log/syslog	Finds specific events in logs.

Note: Use tools like logwatch to automate log analysis.

Warning: Regularly monitor logs to detect unauthorized activity promptly.

Real-Life Scenarios

Scenario 1: Securing a Public Web Server

- **Problem**: A web server is exposed to the internet and vulnerable to attacks.
- **Solution**:
  1. Enable the firewall:
     - Command: sudo ufw enable
  2. Allow only necessary traffic:
     - HTTP: sudo ufw allow 80
     - HTTPS: sudo ufw allow 443
     - SSH: sudo ufw allow ssh
  3. Use SELinux to enforce access policies:
     - Set SELinux to enforcing mode: sudo setenforce 1.
  4. Monitor logs for unusual activity:
     - Command: sudo journalctl -u nginx.

Scenario 2: Preventing Unauthorized File Changes

- **Problem**: Files in a sensitive directory are being modified without authorization.
- **Solution**:

1. Set up AIDE:
   - Initialize the database: sudo aide --init.
   - Rename the database: sudo mv /var/lib/aide/aide.db.new /var/lib/aide/aide.db.
2. Schedule regular checks:
   - Add to cron: 0 1 * * * /usr/sbin/aide --check.
3. Review changes and take corrective actions.

Common Security Mistakes

Mistake 1: Weak Passwords

- **Impact**: Increases the risk of unauthorized access.
- **Solution**:
  o Enforce password complexity:
    - Install pam_pwquality: sudo apt install libpam-pwquality.
    - Configure /etc/security/pwquality.conf:
      - Example: minlen=12 and minclass=3.

Mistake 2: Open Ports

- **Impact**: Exposes the system to unnecessary risks.
- **Solution**:
  1. List open ports:
     - Command: sudo netstat -tuln or ss -tuln.
  2. Close unused ports:
     - Command: sudo ufw deny port_number.

Mistake 3: Ignoring Log Monitoring

- **Impact**: Misses signs of potential breaches.
- **Solution**:
  o Automate log analysis:
    - Install Logwatch: sudo apt install logwatch.
    - Schedule log summaries via cron.

Mistake 4: Misconfigured Firewalls

- **Impact**: May block legitimate traffic or leave gaps for attackers.
- **Solution**:
  o Verify firewall rules:
    - Use sudo ufw status verbose.
  o Test configurations in a staging environment before

applying to production.

Mistake 5: Overlooking Software Updates

- **Impact**: Leaves vulnerabilities unpatched.
- **Solution**:
  - Enable automatic updates:
    - Add to cron: 0 3 * * * apt update && apt upgrade -y.

Note: Regular audits can help identify and resolve these common mistakes.

Best Practices

1. **Apply Principle of Least Privilege**:
   - Limit user permissions to the minimum required for their roles.
   - Use tools like sudo to restrict administrative access and log actions.

2. **Regular Backups**:
   - Ensure critical data is backed up regularly to an external or cloud storage location.
   - Verify backups periodically to ensure they can be restored successfully.

3. **Enforce Strong Password Policies**:
   - Require users to create complex passwords with a minimum length and character diversity.
   - Use tools like pam_pwquality to enforce these policies.
   - Example: Set minlen=12 and minclass=3 to enforce password strength requirements, ensuring secure user accounts.

Chapter 12: Automating Tasks with Scripting

Chapter Overview

This chapter delves into automating repetitive tasks using Bash scripting. It introduces scripting fundamentals, demonstrates practical examples, and explores task scheduling with cron and at. Debugging techniques and best practices are also included to ensure scripts run smoothly and effectively.

The Role of Automation

Automation in Linux:

- Reduces manual effort for repetitive tasks.
- Improves system efficiency and reliability.
- Minimizes the risk of human error in administrative processes.

Key Characteristics of Bash Scripting

Bash scripting provides:

- A powerful way to execute complex tasks automatically.
- Integration with system commands for seamless functionality.
- Support for variables, loops, and conditionals to create dynamic scripts.

Basics of Bash Scripting

What is Bash Scripting?

Bash scripting involves writing a series of commands in a file to automate tasks. These scripts run in the Bash shell, a common command-line interface for Linux.

Writing Your First Bash Script

1. Create a new file:
2. nano myscript.sh
3. Add the shebang line:
4. #!/bin/bash
5. Write a simple script:
6. echo "Hello, World!"
7. Save and exit, then make the script executable:

8. chmod +x myscript.sh
9. Run the script:
10. ./myscript.sh

Understanding Variables in Bash
- Define variables:
- MY_VAR="Hello"
- Use variables:
- echo $MY_VAR

Using Loops in Scripts
- **For Loops**:
- for i in {1..5}; do
-     echo "Iteration $i"
- done
- **While Loops**:
- count=1
- while [$count -le 5]; do
-     echo "Count is $count"
-     ((count++))
- done

Adding Comments to Scripts
- Use # for comments:
- # This is a comment
- echo "Script running"

Note: Comments improve script readability and maintainability.

Automating Administrative Tasks
Common Administrative Tasks to Automate
- File backups.
- Log management.
- Sending email alerts for system events.

Example Scripts for File Backups
- A script to back up /data daily:
- #!/bin/bash
- BACKUP_DIR="/backup"
- SOURCE_DIR="/data"
- DATE=$(date +%F)

- tar -czf $BACKUP_DIR/backup_$DATE.tar.gz $SOURCE_DIR
- echo "Backup completed for $DATE"

Automating Log Management

- Rotate and archive logs:
- #!/bin/bash
- LOG_DIR="/var/log"
- ARCHIVE_DIR="/log_archive"
- tar -czf $ARCHIVE_DIR/logs_$(date +%F).tar.gz $LOG_DIR/*
- echo "Logs archived."

Sending Automated Email Alerts

- Script to send email alerts for high disk usage:
- #!/bin/bash
- THRESHOLD=80
- USAGE=$(df / | grep / | awk '{print $5}' | sed 's/%//')
- if [$USAGE -gt $THRESHOLD]; then
-     echo "Disk usage is at $USAGE%" | mail -s "Disk Usage Alert" admin@example.com
- fi

Scheduling with Cron and At

What is a Cron Job?

Cron jobs schedule tasks to run at specified times or intervals.

Creating and Managing Cron Jobs

1. Edit the cron table:
2. crontab -e
3. Add a job to run a script daily at midnight:
4. 0 0 * * * /path/to/script.sh
5. View scheduled jobs:
6. crontab -l

Understanding Cron Syntax

- Format: minute hour day month day_of_week command
- Example:
  - Run a script every Monday at 8 AM:
  - 0 8 * * 1 /path/to/script.sh

Scheduling One-Time Tasks with At

1. Install at if not already installed:
2. sudo apt install at
3. Schedule a task:
4. echo "shutdown now" | at 22:00
5. View pending jobs:
6. atq
7. Remove a job:
8. atrm <job_id>

Monitoring and Debugging Scheduled Jobs

Troubleshooting Scripts

- Use set -x at the start of a script to enable debugging:
- #!/bin/bash
- set -x
- echo "Debugging enabled"
- Use set +x to disable debugging:
- set +x

Debugging Bash Scripts

- Test scripts manually before scheduling.
- Check syntax errors:
- bash -n script.sh
- Run the script in verbose mode:
- bash -x script.sh

Common Scripting Errors and Fixes

- **Error**: "Permission denied"
  - o **Fix**: Make the script executable:
  - o chmod +x script.sh
- **Error**: "Command not found"
  - o **Fix**: Check for typos or ensure the required program is installed.
- **Error**: "No such file or directory"
  - o **Fix**: Verify file paths in the script.

Best Practices

1. **Use Descriptive Variable Names**:

   o Example: Use BACKUP_DIR instead of DIR.

2. **Test Scripts Thoroughly**:
   o Test scripts in a safe environment before deployment.

3. **Document Your Scripts**:
   o Add comments to explain complex logic.

4. **Keep Scripts Secure**:
   o Set proper permissions to restrict access.
   o Avoid storing sensitive data (e.g., passwords) in plain text.

5. **Leverage Modular Scripting**:
   o Break large scripts into smaller, reusable functions.

By mastering Bash scripting and scheduling, you can automate repetitive tasks and streamline Linux system management effectively.

Chapter 13: Advanced Linux Administration

Chapter Overview

This chapter explores advanced administration techniques in Linux, including virtualization and containerization. You'll learn how to set up and manage virtual machines with KVM and QEMU, utilize Docker containers for lightweight application deployment, and handle advanced features like nested virtualization and multi-container applications with Docker Compose.

The Role of Advanced Administration

Advanced administration in Linux focuses on:

- Optimizing resources using virtualization and containers.
- Enhancing scalability and flexibility in system management.
- Leveraging tools to streamline complex administrative tasks.

Key Characteristics of Virtualization and Containers

Virtualization

- **Definition**: Allows multiple virtual machines (VMs) to run on a single physical host.
- **Purpose**: Enables resource allocation and isolation for diverse workloads.
- **Use Cases**: Testing, development, and production environments.

Containers

- **Definition**: Provide lightweight and efficient application isolation.
- **Benefits**: Use shared operating systems for reduced overhead compared to VMs.
- **Use Cases**: Application deployment and microservices architecture.

Virtualization with Linux

What is Virtualization?

Virtualization is the creation of virtual versions of hardware resources, enabling multiple operating systems to run concurrently on a single machine.

Benefits of Using Virtualization in Linux

- **Resource Efficiency**: Maximizes utilization of physical hardware.
- **Isolation**: Keeps environments separate, reducing risk.
- **Flexibility**: Easily deploy and manage different OSes and applications.

Setting Up KVM and QEMU

Installing Virtualization Tools

1. Install KVM and QEMU:
2. sudo apt install qemu-kvm libvirt-daemon-system libvirt-clients bridge-utils virt-manager
3. Verify installation:
4. kvm-ok

Creating Virtual Machines

1. Launch virt-manager (GUI tool):
2. virt-manager
3. Follow the wizard to:
   - Select installation media (ISO file).
   - Allocate CPU, memory, and disk space.

Managing Virtual Machines

- Start a VM:
- virsh start vm_name
- Stop a VM:
- virsh shutdown vm_name
- Pause a VM:
- virsh suspend vm_name

Allocating Resources to VMs

- Adjust CPU and memory allocation dynamically:
- virsh setvcpus vm_name 4 --config
- virsh setmem vm_name 2048M --config

Introduction to Docker Containers

What are Containers?

Containers are lightweight environments that package applications and their dependencies, ensuring consistency across development and production.

Docker vs. Traditional Virtualization

Feature	Docker	Virtualization
Overhead	Low	High
Isolation	Application-level	Full OS-level
Startup Time	Seconds	Minutes

Installing Docker on Linux

1. Update the system:
2. sudo apt update
3. Install Docker:
4. sudo apt install docker.io
5. Enable and start Docker:
6. sudo systemctl enable --now docker

Managing Containers with Docker CLI

Pulling and Running Containers

- Pull an image:
- docker pull nginx
- Run a container:
- docker run -d -p 80:80 --name webserver nginx

Stopping and Removing Containers

- Stop a container:
- docker stop webserver
- Remove a container:
- docker rm webserver

Inspecting Container Logs and Performance

- View logs:
- docker logs webserver
- Monitor performance:
- docker stats

Advanced Topics in Virtualization and Containers

Setting Up Nested Virtualization

- Enable nested virtualization:
- sudo modprobe kvm_intel nested=1
- Verify:
- cat /sys/module/kvm_intel/parameters/nested

- Use nested virtualization for running VMs inside VMs for testing and development.

Using Docker Compose for Multi-Container Applications

1. Install Docker Compose:
2. sudo apt install docker-compose
3. Create a docker-compose.yml file:
4. version: '3.8'
5. services:
6.   web:
7.   image: nginx
8.   ports:
9.   - "80:80"
10. db:
11.   image: mysql
12.   environment:
13.   MYSQL_ROOT_PASSWORD: example
14. Deploy the application:
15. docker-compose up -d
16. Manage the application:
    o Stop:
    o docker-compose down

Real-Life Scenarios

Scenario 1: Hosting a Multi-Tier Application with Docker Compose

- **Problem**: Deploying a web application with separate services for the frontend, backend, and database.
- **Solution**:
  1. Create a docker-compose.yml file with services for each tier:
  2. version: '3.8'
  3. services:
  4.   frontend:
  5.   image: react-app
  6.   ports:
  7.   - "3000:3000"
  8.   backend:

9.   image: node-api
10.   ports:
11.   - "5000:5000"
12.   db:
13.   image: postgres
14.   environment:
15.   POSTGRES_PASSWORD: example
16. Deploy the application:
17. docker-compose up -d
18. Verify that all services are running:
19. docker-compose ps

Scenario 2: Creating a Test Environment with Nested Virtualization

- **Problem**: Setting up a virtualized test environment for software development.
- **Solution**:
  1. Enable nested virtualization:
  2. sudo modprobe kvm_intel nested=1
  3. Create a VM using virt-manager.
  4. Inside the VM, install KVM and set up additional virtual machines.

Common Mistakes and Fixes

Mistake 1: Docker Container Fails to Start

- **Cause**: Missing or incorrect configurations in docker-compose.yml.
- **Solution**:
  1. Check the configuration file syntax:
  2. docker-compose config
  3. Inspect logs for errors:
  4. docker-compose logs

Mistake 2: VM Performance Issues

- **Cause**: Over-allocation of host resources.
- **Solution**:
  1. Monitor resource usage:
  2. top
  3. Adjust VM resource allocation using virsh:
  4. virsh setvcpus vm_name 2 --config

5. virsh setmem vm_name 2048M --config

Mistake 3: Nested Virtualization Not Working

- **Cause**: Nested virtualization not enabled on the host.
- **Solution**:
    - Verify nested support:
    - cat /sys/module/kvm_intel/parameters/nested
    - Enable nested virtualization if needed.

Performance Monitoring

Monitoring Virtual Machines

- Use virt-top for real-time resource monitoring:
- sudo virt-top
- Check VM-specific statistics with virsh domstats:
- virsh domstats vm_name

Monitoring Containers

- Use docker stats for live container metrics:
- docker stats
- Integrate monitoring with tools like Prometheus and Grafana for advanced analytics.

Host Performance Monitoring

- Use htop for a graphical view of system resource usage:
- htop
- Analyze disk I/O with iostat:
- iostat -x

Best Practices

1. **Monitor Resource Usage**:
    - Use tools like top, htop, or docker stats.
2. **Document Configurations**:
    - Maintain records of VM and container configurations.
3. **Secure Virtualization and Containers**:
    - Enable authentication for virt-manager.
    - Use Docker security features like docker scan for vulnerabilities.
4. **Test Before Deployment**:
    - Validate container images and VMs in a staging environment.

5. **Regular Updates**:
    o Update virtualization tools and container images to mitigate vulnerabilities.

By mastering advanced Linux administration, including virtualization and containers, you can optimize resources, improve scalability, and enhance system reliability.

Chapter 14: Troubleshooting and Problem Solving

Chapter Overview

This chapter delves into identifying and resolving issues in Linux systems. It covers techniques for debugging boot failures, diagnosing network problems, and detecting hardware issues. Practical tools and methods are provided to help system administrators maintain system reliability and performance.

The Role of Troubleshooting

Effective troubleshooting ensures:

- Minimal downtime by quickly identifying and resolving issues.
- Enhanced system reliability through proactive problem-solving.
- Comprehensive understanding of system behavior under different conditions.

Key Characteristics of Problem-Solving Tools

- **Efficiency**: Provide quick and actionable insights.
- **Precision**: Help pinpoint the root cause of issues.
- **Flexibility**: Adaptable for different scenarios, such as boot failures or hardware diagnostics.

Debugging Boot Issues

Common Causes of Boot Failures

Boot issues often stem from a variety of factors. Here are common causes:

- **Corrupted Bootloader Configurations**: This can occur after updates or improper configuration changes.

- **Missing or Damaged Kernel Files**: Deleting critical kernel files or failed updates can lead to boot failures.
- **Misconfigured System Partitions**: Errors in partition tables or incorrect mounts in /etc/fstab can disrupt boot processes.

Note: GRUB rescue mode is a powerful tool but requires careful handling to avoid additional issues.

Using GRUB Rescue Mode

1. Access GRUB rescue mode by pressing Esc during boot.
2. Identify available partitions:
3. ls
4. Locate the boot partition and set it:
5. set root=(hd0,msdos1)
6. Load the kernel and initramfs manually:
7. linux /vmlinuz root=/dev/sda1 ro
8. initrd /initrd.img
9. boot

Warning: Incorrect GRUB reinstallation can make your system unbootable. Double-check commands before execution.

Restoring Default Boot Settings

Restoring boot settings involves reinitializing the bootloader and ensuring kernel files are intact:

1. **Boot into a Live CD/USB**:
   o Use a bootable Linux distribution to access the system.
2. **Reinstall GRUB**:
3. sudo grub-install /dev/sda
4. sudo update-grub
5. **Repair Corrupted Kernel Files**:
   o Mount the root partition:
   o sudo mount /dev/sda1 /mnt
   o Reinstall the kernel:
   o sudo chroot /mnt
   o sudo apt install --reinstall linux-image-$(uname -r)
6. Restart the system and verify functionality.

Diagnosing Network Problems
Tools for Network Troubleshooting

ping: Tests connectivity to a remote host.

traceroute: Traces the path packets take to a destination.

Wireshark: Analyzes network traffic at a granular level.

Using ping to Check Connectivity

Note: Use ping cautiously in networks with restrictive policies as excessive usage might trigger alerts.

Test connection to a host:

ping -c 4 example.com

Analyze the output for packet loss and latency.

Diagnosing Issues with traceroute

Traceroute helps identify delays and failures in packet delivery paths:

Trace the route to a destination:

traceroute example.com

Analyze the hops:

Look for high latency or timeouts.

Identify problematic nodes based on their IPs or hostnames.

Test alternative routes using mtr (if installed):

sudo mtr example.com

Warning: Wireshark captures sensitive data. Ensure you have proper authorization before using it on a network.

Analyzing Packets with Wireshark

Install Wireshark:

sudo apt install wireshark

Capture packets on a specific interface:

sudo wireshark

Filter results for specific protocols or IP addresses.

Common Network Issues and Fixes

Issue: "Network unreachable"

Fix: Check IP configuration with ip addr and adjust settings.

Issue: DNS resolution failure

Fix: Update /etc/resolv.conf with the correct DNS server.

Identifying Hardware Failures

Symptoms of Hardware Issues

Hardware failures can manifest in various ways. Common symptoms include:

Unusual Noises: Clicking or grinding sounds from hard drives may indicate impending failure.

System Crashes or Freezes: Frequent crashes, especially under load, may point to memory or CPU issues.

Error Logs: Messages like "disk I/O error" or "device not responding" in system logs.

Performance Degradation: Slow read/write speeds or frequent retries in tasks involving disk access.

Checking System Logs for Clues

View logs in /var/log or use journalctl:

sudo journalctl -p err

Look for hardware-related errors, such as disk I/O failures.

Using smartctl to Test Hard Drives

Command	Description
sudo smartctl -H	Checks the overall health of a drive.
sudo smartctl -t	Runs a detailed test on the specified drive.

Note: SMART tests might take a while to complete. Schedule them during maintenance windows.

Install smartmontools:

sudo apt install smartmontools

Check the health of a drive:

sudo smartctl -H /dev/sda

Run a detailed test:

sudo smartctl -t long /dev/sda

Warning: Handling hardware components improperly can cause damage or void warranties. Use anti-static precautions.

Replacing Faulty Hardware Safely

Follow these steps to replace hardware components without causing further damage:

Backup Critical Data:

Use tools like rsync or dd to ensure data safety.

Power Off the System:

Disconnect the system from all power sources to avoid electrical damage.

Use Proper Handling Tools:

Wear an anti-static wrist strap to prevent static electricity damage.

Install the New Component:
Ensure connectors are firmly secured to avoid loose connections.
Power On and Verify:
Run diagnostic tools like dmesg or lshw to confirm the hardware is functioning correctly.

Best Practices
Document Known Issues:
Maintain a log of past problems and their resolutions.
Use Diagnostic Tools Regularly:
Schedule periodic checks with tools like smartctl and ping.
Train on Troubleshooting Skills:
Practice common scenarios in a controlled environment.
Perform Root Cause Analysis:
Address underlying causes to prevent recurring issues.
Maintain a Spare Hardware Inventory:
Keep essential components on hand for quick replacements.
By mastering these troubleshooting techniques and leveraging the right tools, you can ensure your Linux systems remain reliable and efficient.

Chapter 15: Essential Tools for Administrators

Chapter Overview
This chapter explores the indispensable tools Linux administrators rely on to manage, troubleshoot, and maintain systems. From text editors to monitoring and backup utilities, these tools form the backbone of effective Linux administration.

The Role of Essential Tools
- Essential tools empower administrators to:
- Perform routine tasks efficiently.
- Address system issues proactively.
- Simplify complex administrative processes.

Key Characteristics of Administrative Utilities

Administrative utilities share these traits:

Simplicity: Designed for ease of use.

Versatility: Applicable across a wide range of tasks.

Reliability: Proven performance in critical scenarios.

Text Editors: Vim and Nano

Why Use Vim and Nano?

Vim:

- Powerful and highly configurable.
- Ideal for advanced editing tasks and automation.

Nano:

- Simple and beginner-friendly.
- Useful for quick edits in terminal environments.

Basic Vim Commands

- Vim is highly versatile, and mastering its basic commands can significantly improve efficiency.
- Enter command mode:
- Press Esc. This is the default mode for issuing commands.
- Open a file:
- vim filename
- Replace filename with the desired file name.
- Insert text:
- Press i to enter insert mode, allowing text editing.
- Save and exit:
- Press Esc to switch to command mode and type :wq to save changes and quit.

Tip: Use :help in Vim to access detailed documentation and tutorials.

Advanced Vim Shortcuts

- Delete an entire line:
- Press dd.
- Copy a line:
- Press yy.
- Paste a copied line:

- Press p.
- Undo the last change:
- Press u.
- Search for a word:
- Type /word and press Enter.

Note: Practice these commands in a test file to build confidence.

Enter command mode:
- Press Esc.
- Open a file:
- vim filename
- Insert text:
- Press i to enter insert mode.
- Save and exit:
- Press Esc and type :wq.

Tip: Use :help in Vim to access the built-in manual.

Getting Started with Nano

Nano is an excellent choice for beginners, offering a straightforward interface for text editing.

Open a file:
- nano filename
- Replace filename with the desired file name.
- Edit text directly using your keyboard.
- Save changes:
- Press Ctrl+O, then press Enter to confirm the file name.
- Exit Nano:
- Press Ctrl+X.

Additional Nano Shortcuts

- Cut text:
- Use Ctrl+K to cut the current line.
- Paste text:
- Use Ctrl+U to paste the cut text.
- Search for text:
- Use Ctrl+W, type the search term, and press Enter.
- Display help:
- Use Ctrl+G to view Nano's built-in help menu.

Tip: Nano's simplicity makes it ideal for quick edits, especially on remote servers.

Open a file:

- nano filename
- Edit text directly.
- Save changes:
- Press Ctrl+O.
- Exit:
- Press Ctrl+X.

File Transfer: SCP and Rsync

What is SCP?

SCP (Secure Copy Protocol) is a command-line utility for transferring files securely over SSH.

Transferring Files Securely with SCP

Copy a file to a remote server:

- scp file.txt user@remote:/path/to/destination

Copy a file from a remote server:

- scp user@remote:/path/to/file.txt /local/destination

Transfer directories recursively:

- scp -r /local/dir user@remote:/remote/dir

Introduction to Rsync: Synchronizing Files

Rsync is a versatile tool for file synchronization and backup.

Using Rsync for Backups

Rsync is a robust and flexible utility for efficient file synchronization and backup.

Synchronize local directories:

- rsync -av /source/dir /destination/dir
- The -a flag ensures all attributes (permissions, timestamps) are preserved.
- The -v flag enables verbose output for detailed progress.

Sync files to a remote server:

- rsync -avz /local/dir user@remote:/remote/dir
- The -z flag compresses data during transfer, improving speed over slower networks.

Use dry-run mode to preview changes:
- rsync -avz --dry-run /source /destination
- This allows you to verify actions before making changes

Advanced Rsync Features

Delete files at the destination not present in the source:
- rsync -av --delete /source/dir /destination/dir
- Exclude specific files or directories:
- rsync -av --exclude 'file_or_dir' /source /destination

Note: Rsync supports incremental backups, reducing the amount of data transferred by copying only changed files.

Synchronize local directories:
- rsync -av /source/dir /destination/dir

Sync files to a remote server:
- rsync -avz /local/dir user@remote:/remote/dir

Use dry-run mode to preview changes:
- rsync -avz --dry-run /source /destination

Monitoring Tools: Nagios and Zabbix

What is Nagios?

Nagios is a powerful monitoring system for network and infrastructure.

Setting Up Basic Monitoring with Nagios

Nagios provides a robust platform for real-time monitoring of system and network health.

Install Nagios:

Update package repositories:
- sudo apt update

Install Nagios Core:
- sudo apt install nagios

Configure Services to Monitor:

Open the main configuration file:
- sudo nano /etc/nagios/nagios.cfg
- Define host and service objects in configuration files located in /etc/nagios/conf.d/.

Restart the Nagios Service:

sudo systemctl restart nagios

Access the Web Interface:
- Navigate to http://<server-ip>/nagios in a web browser.

Key Features to Monitor:
- Host availability.
- Service uptime (e.g., HTTP, SSH).
- Resource usage (CPU, memory).

Note: Nagios requires Apache for its web interface. Ensure it is installed and running.

Install Nagios:
- sudo apt install nagios

Configure services to monitor:
- Edit /etc/nagios/nagios.cfg.

Restart the Nagios service:
- sudo systemctl restart nagios

Introduction to Zabbix: Advanced Monitoring

Zabbix offers comprehensive monitoring for large-scale infrastructures.

Configuring Alerts and Notifications

Set up email alerts:
- Configure SMTP settings in Zabbix.

Create triggers for specific conditions:

Example: High CPU usage.

Test notification functionality to ensure reliability.

Backup Utilities: Bacula and Amanda

Overview of Bacula: Enterprise Backup Solutions

Bacula is designed for scalable, automated backups across multiple systems.

Setting Up Bacula for Automatic Backups

Bacula is a sophisticated backup solution ideal for enterprise environments.

Install Bacula Components:

Install the server and client packages:
- sudo apt install bacula-server bacula-client

Configure Bacula Director:
Edit /etc/bacula/bacula-dir.conf to define backup jobs, file sets, and storage devices.

Start the Bacula Services:
- sudo systemctl start bacula-dir
- sudo systemctl start bacula-fd
- sudo systemctl start bacula-sd

Schedule Automatic Backups:
Define schedules in the Bacula Director configuration file:

```
Schedule {
   Name = "DailyBackup"
   Run = Level=Full Pool=Daily at 01:00
```

Advantages of Bacula:
- Supports multiple backup types (full, incremental, differential).

Centralized management of backup jobs.

Tip: Use Bacula's web interface (Bweb) for easier configuration and monitoring.

Install Bacula components:
- sudo apt install bacula-server bacula-client
- Configure backup jobs in /etc/bacula/bacula-dir.conf.
- Start the Bacula service:
- sudo systemctl start bacula

Amanda Basics: Simplifying Backup Processes
Amanda (Advanced Maryland Automatic Network Disk Archiver) simplifies backups by centralizing management.

Install Amanda:
- sudo apt install amanda-server amanda-client

Configure the backup environment:
- Edit /etc/amanda/amanda.conf.

Run backups:
- amdump config_name

Comparing Bacula and Amanda for Different Use Cases

Feature	Bacula	Amanda
Scalability	High (suitable for enterprises)	Moderate (ideal for small setups)

Feature	Bacula	Amanda
Complexity	Requires detailed configuration	Simple setup and management
Flexibility	Supports diverse storage types	Focused on disk and tape backups

Best Practices

Master Text Editors:

- Learn advanced Vim techniques for efficiency.

Secure File Transfers:

- Use SCP and Rsync over encrypted connections.

Proactive Monitoring:

- Regularly review monitoring dashboards and alerts.

Automate Backups:

- Schedule regular backups with Bacula or Amanda.

Test Configurations:

- Validate settings for all tools in a staging environment.

By leveraging these essential tools, administrators can enhance their efficiency and ensure robust Linux system management.

Chapter 16: Virtualization and Cloud Administration

Chapter Overview

This chapter introduces virtualization technologies and cloud administration. It explores key concepts, tools, and techniques for setting up virtual machines and managing cloud environments like AWS and OpenStack.

The Role of Virtualization

Virtualization plays a pivotal role in modern IT by:

- Reducing hardware costs through efficient resource utilization.
- Improving scalability and flexibility in deploying applications.
- Enhancing disaster recovery and system testing capabilities.

Key Characteristics of Cloud Platforms

- **Elasticity**: Scales resources up or down based on demand.
- **Cost Efficiency**: Pay-as-you-go pricing models.
- **Accessibility**: Global access to resources via the internet.
- **Automation**: Automates resource provisioning and management.

Understanding Virtualization Technologies
What is Virtualization?
Virtualization is the process of creating virtual instances of hardware, allowing multiple operating systems to run concurrently on a single physical machine.

Types of Virtualization
1. **Full Virtualization**:
    a. Uses hypervisors like VMware or KVM.
    b. Provides complete isolation between virtual machines.
2. **Paravirtualization**:
    a. Requires modified guest operating systems for better performance.
3. **Hardware-Assisted Virtualization**:
    a. Leverages CPU extensions like Intel VT-x or AMD-V for efficiency.

Introduction to Hypervisors
1. **KVM (Kernel-based Virtual Machine)**:
    a. Open-source hypervisor for Linux.
2. **VMware**:
    a. Proprietary solutions like VMware Workstation and ESXi.
3. **Others**:
    a. Examples include Xen and Microsoft Hyper-V.

Advantages and Use Cases of Virtualization
- **Server Consolidation**: Run multiple servers on a single machine.
- **Testing Environments**: Isolated environments for software testing.
- **Disaster Recovery**: Simplifies backup and recovery processes.

Setting Up KVM for Linux
Real-Life Scenario
Many IT departments use KVM to host development environments, allowing developers to test applications in isolated virtual machines without impacting production systems.

Note: Ensure your system supports virtualization by enabling VT-x or AMD-V in the BIOS/UEFI settings before proceeding.

Installing and Configuring KVM

1. Install required packages: `sudo apt update`
   `sudo apt install qemu-kvm libvirt-daemon-system`

```
libvirt-clients virt-manager
```

2. Verify KVM installation: kvm-ok
3. Enable and start the libvirt service: `sudo systemctl enable --now libvirtd`

Creating and Managing Virtual Machines

1. Launch virt-manager (GUI tool): `virt-manager`
2. Follow the wizard to:
    a. Select installation media (ISO file).
    b. Allocate CPU, memory, and disk space.

Allocating CPU, Memory, and Storage to VMs

- Adjust resources dynamically using virsh: `virsh setvcpus vm_name 4 --config`
  `virsh setmem vm_name 2048M --config`

Snapshots and Cloning of Virtual Machines

Warning: Snapshots consume disk space. Regularly review and delete unused snapshots to manage storage efficiently.

1. Create a snapshot: `virsh snapshot-create-as vm_name snapshot_name`

2. Clone a VM: `virt-clone --original vm_name --name new_vm --file /path/to/new_disk.img`

VMware Basics
Real-Life Scenario
Many small businesses use VMware Workstation to simulate enterprise environments for training IT staff on virtualization without the need for expensive hardware setups.

Troubleshooting Tips

- **Problem**: Virtual machines are slow to respond.
  - **Solution**: Verify that the host system has sufficient resources and adjust the allocated CPU and memory settings for the virtual machine.
- **Problem**: USB devices not recognized in VMware Workstation.
  - **Solution**: Ensure the VMware Tools package is installed and the USB controller is enabled in the VM settings.

Overview of VMware Products

- **VMware Workstation**: A desktop hypervisor for running multiple operating systems.
- **VMware ESXi**: Enterprise-grade hypervisor for server virtualization.

Setting Up VMware Workstation for Linux

1. Download the VMware Workstation installer from the official site.
2. Make the installer executable: `chmod +x VMware-Workstation-Full-*.bundle`

3. Run the installer: `sudo ./VMware-Workstation-Full-*.bundle`

Configuring Virtual Machines in VMware

1. Create a new VM:
   a. Follow the wizard to set up OS, hardware resources, and disk space.
2. Manage VM snapshots:
   a. Take snapshots before critical updates or changes.

Introduction to Cloud Platforms

What is Cloud Computing?

Cloud computing delivers computing services like storage, servers, and applications over the internet.

Types of Cloud Services

1. **Infrastructure as a Service (IaaS)**:
    a. Provides virtualized computing resources.
    b. Examples: AWS EC2, Google Compute Engine.
2. **Platform as a Service (PaaS)**:
    a. Offers development platforms and tools.
    b. Examples: AWS Elastic Beanstalk, Heroku.
3. **Software as a Service (SaaS)**:
    a. Delivers software applications via the internet.
    b. Examples: Google Workspace, Microsoft Office 365.

Public vs. Private vs. Hybrid Clouds

Type	Description	Example
Public	Services shared across multiple tenants.	AWS, Azure, Google Cloud
Private	Dedicated resources for a single entity.	On-premises OpenStack
Hybrid	Combines public and private cloud models.	AWS Outposts

AWS and OpenStack Administration

Real-Life Scenario: AWS Cloud Usage

A startup deploys a web application on AWS using EC2 instances to handle varying traffic loads efficiently with auto-scaling groups.

Troubleshooting Tips

- **Problem**: Unable to SSH into an EC2 instance.
    - **Solution**: Verify that the correct security group allows inbound traffic on port 22 and ensure the private key

matches the instance's key pair.

Real-Life Scenario: OpenStack in Academia

A university deploys OpenStack to provide students with virtualized labs for hands-on learning in a controlled environment.

Troubleshooting Tips

- **Problem**: Dashboard inaccessible after deployment.
  - o **Solution**: Check the Apache and OpenStack services. Restart services if necessary: `sudo systemctl restart apache2`
    `sudo systemctl restart openstack-dashboard`

Introduction to AWS: Key Services for Beginners

1. **Compute**:
   a. EC2 for virtual servers.
2. **Storage**:
   a. S3 for object storage.
3. **Database**:
   a. RDS for managed databases.

Setting Up EC2 Instances on AWS

Real-Life Scenario: A startup deploys a web application on AWS using EC2 instances to handle varying traffic loads efficiently with auto-scaling groups.

Troubleshooting Tips:

- **Problem**: Unable to SSH into an EC2 instance.
  - o **Solution**: Verify that the correct security group allows inbound traffic on port 22 and ensure the private key matches the instance's key pair.

1. Log in to the AWS Management Console.
2. Navigate to the EC2 Dashboard.
3. Launch an instance:
   a. Select an AMI (Amazon Machine Image).
   b. Choose instance type (e.g., t2.micro).
   c. Configure security groups and key pairs.
4. Access the instance via SSH: `ssh -i key.pem ec2-user@<public-ip>`

Overview of OpenStack: Open Source Cloud Solutions

Real-Life Scenario: A university deploys OpenStack to provide students with virtualized labs for hands-on learning in a controlled environment.

Troubleshooting Tips:

- **Problem**: Dashboard inaccessible after deployment.
    - o **Solution**: Check the Apache and OpenStack services. Restart services if necessary: `sudo systemctl restart apache2`
    `sudo systemctl restart openstack-dashboard`

OpenStack is a suite of tools for building and managing private and public clouds.

Installing and Configuring OpenStack

1. Install the OpenStack client: `sudo apt update`
`sudo apt install python3-openstackclient`
2. Deploy OpenStack using DevStack for testing: `git clone https://opendev.org/openstack/devstack`
`cd devstack`
`./stack.sh`

3. Access the OpenStack dashboard:
    a. Navigate to `http://<server-ip>/dashboard`.

Best Practices

1. **Monitor Resource Utilization**:
    a. Use tools like `virt-top` for VMs and AWS CloudWatch for cloud resources.
2. **Secure Virtual Environments**:
    a. Enable two-factor authentication and secure key management.
3. **Plan Backup and Disaster Recovery**:
    a. Use AWS Backup or OpenStack Swift for critical data.
4. **Optimize Costs**:
    a. Regularly review resource usage and terminate unused instances.
5. **Document Configurations**:
    a. Maintain detailed records of virtual and cloud setups for future reference.

By mastering virtualization and cloud administration, you can build scalable, efficient, and secure IT environments.

.

Chapter 17: Web and Database Servers

Chapter Overview

This chapter explores the foundational elements of web and database servers. It includes setting up and managing Apache and Nginx for web hosting and using MySQL and PostgreSQL for database management. Security practices and backup strategies for these servers are also covered.

The Role of Web and Database Servers

Web and database servers are essential components of modern IT infrastructure. They support:

- Hosting websites and applications accessible over the internet.
- Storing and managing data securely and efficiently.
- Enabling scalable and reliable digital solutions.

Key Characteristics of Server Management

1. **Reliability**: Ensuring servers remain operational 24/7.
2. **Scalability**: Ability to handle increased traffic and data demand
3. **Security**: Protecting servers from unauthorized access and thr
4. **Ease of Configuration**: Simplifying deployment and manager processes.

Setting Up Apache and Nginx

What is a Web Server?

A web server is software that processes and delivers web co over the internet. Apache and Nginx are two of the most pc

Installing Apache on Linux

Apache is one of the most widely used web servers, known for its flexibility and reliability.

1. Update the system to ensure all packages are current: `sudo apt update`

2. Install Apache: `sudo apt install apache2`

3. Start and enable the Apache service to ensure it runs on boot:
   `sudo systemctl start apache2`
   `sudo systemctl enable apache2`

4. Test the installation by opening a web browser and navigating to `http://<server-ip>`.

The default web directory for Apache is `/var/www/html`. Place your files here to host them.

date the system: `sudo apt update`

`pache: `sudo apt install apache2`

able the Apache service: `sudo systemctl start`

`mctl enable apache2`

b server often used for load balancing and

the latest package information: `sudo`

2. Install Nginx: `sudo apt install nginx`

3. Start and enable the Nginx service to run on startup: `sudo systemctl start nginx`
`sudo systemctl enable nginx`

4. Verify the installation by navigating to `http://<server-ip>` in a web browser.

Note: The default web directory for Nginx is `/var/www/html`. Ensure proper permissions for any uploaded files.

1. Update the system: `sudo apt update`

2. Install Nginx: `sudo apt install nginx`

3. Start and enable the Nginx service: `sudo systemctl start nginx`
`sudo systemctl enable nginx`

Configuring Virtual Hosts for Apache

Virtual hosts allow multiple websites to run on a single Apache server.

1. Create a directory for your website:

```
sudo mkdir -p /var/www/example.com
```

2. Set the correct permissions:

```
sudo chown -R $USER:$USER /var/www/example.com
sudo chmod -R 755 /var/www
```

3. Create an index file for testing:

```
echo '<h1>Welcome to Example.com</h1>' >
/var/www/example.com/index.html
```

4. Create a virtual host configuration file:

```
sudo nano /etc/apache2/sites-available/example.com.conf
```

Example content:

```
<VirtualHost *:80>
    ServerName example.com
    ServerAlias www.example.com
    DocumentRoot /var/www/example.com
    ErrorLog ${APACHE_LOG_DIR}/error.log
    CustomLog ${APACHE_LOG_DIR}/access.log combined
</VirtualHost>
```

5. Enable the virtual host:

```
sudo a2ensite example.com
```

6. Reload Apache to apply changes:

```
sudo systemctl reload apache2
```

7. Create a virtual host configuration file:

```
sudo nano /etc/apache2/sites-available/example.com.conf
```

Example content:

```
<VirtualHost *:80>
    ServerName example.com
```

```
    DocumentRoot /var/www/example.com
    ErrorLog ${APACHE_LOG_DIR}/error.log
    CustomLog ${APACHE_LOG_DIR}/access.log combined
</VirtualHost>
```

8. Enable the site:

```
sudo a2ensite example.com
```

9. Reload Apache:

```
sudo systemctl reload apache2
```

Configuring Virtual Hosts for Nginx

In Nginx, virtual hosts are referred to as server blocks.

1. Create a directory for your website:

```
sudo mkdir -p /var/www/example.com
```

2. Set the correct permissions:

```
sudo chown -R $USER:$USER /var/www/example.com
sudo chmod -R 755 /var/www
```

3. Create an index file for testing:

```
echo '<h1>Welcome to Example.com</h1>' >
/var/www/example.com/index.html
```

4. Create a server block configuration file:

```
sudo nano /etc/nginx/sites-available/example.com
```

Example content:

```
server {
    listen 80;
    server_name example.com www.example.com;
    root /var/www/example.com;

    location / {
        index index.html;
    }
}
```

5. Enable the site by creating a symbolic link:

```
sudo ln -s /etc/nginx/sites-available/example.com
/etc/nginx/sites-enabled/
```

6. Test the Nginx configuration:

```
sudo nginx -t
```

7. Reload Nginx to apply changes:

```
sudo systemctl reload nginx
```

8. Create a server block configuration file:

```
sudo nano /etc/nginx/sites-available/example.com
```

Example content:

```
server {
    listen 80;
    server_name example.com;
    root /var/www/example.com;

    location / {
        index index.html;
    }
}
```

9. Enable the site:

```
sudo ln -s /etc/nginx/sites-available/example.com
/etc/nginx/sites-enabled/
```

10. Reload Nginx:

```
sudo systemctl reload nginx
```

Managing Databases

What is a Database?

A database is an organized collection of data that can be accessed, managed, and updated efficiently. MySQL and PostgreSQL are widel database management systems (DBMS).

MySQL Basics

1. Install MySQL: `sudo apt install mysql-server`

2. Secure MySQL installation: `sudo mysql_secure_installation`

3. Access the MySQL shell: `sudo mysql`

Creating and Managing Databases in MySQL

1. Create a database: `CREATE DATABASE my_database;`

2. Create a user and grant privileges: `CREATE USER
   'my_user'@'localhost' IDENTIFIED BY 'password';
   GRANT ALL PRIVILEGES ON my_database.* TO
   'my_user'@'localhost';
   FLUSH PRIVILEGES;`

3. View databases: `SHOW DATABASES;`

ʳreSQL Basics

ˈstall PostgreSQL: `sudo apt install postgresql
  ʳtgresql-contrib`

ʰhe PostgreSQL shell: `sudo -i -u postgres psql`

ˈaging Databases in PostgreSQL

ʸ used

ˈse: `CREATE DATABASE my_database;`

ˈsign privileges: `CREATE USER my_user
  assword';`
  `ˈGES ON DATABASE my_database TO`

Securing Web and Database Servers

Enabling HTTPS with SSL Certificates

1. Install Certbot: `sudo apt install certbot python3-certbot-apache`

2. Obtain and install an SSL certificate for Apache: `sudo certbot --apache`

3. For Nginx, use: `sudo certbot --nginx`

Configuring Firewalls for Server Protection

1. Allow HTTP and HTTPS traffic: `sudo ufw allow 'Apache Full'`
`sudo ufw allow 'Nginx Full'`

2. Enable the firewall: `sudo ufw enable`

Regular Backups for Web and Database Servers

1. Backup a MySQL database: `mysqldump -u root -p my_database > my_database_backup.sql`

2. Backup a PostgreSQL database: `pg_dump -U postgres my_database > my_database_backup.sql`

3. Automate backups using Cron:
   a. Add a Cron job: `crontab -e`

   b. Example Cron entry: `0 2 * * *`

```
/usr/bin/mysqldump -u root -p'mypassword'
my_database >
/backups/my_database_backup.sql
```

Best Practices

1. **Keep Software Updated**:
   a. Regularly update Apache, Nginx, MySQL, and PostgreSQL to the latest versions.
2. **Enable Security Features**:
   a. Use firewalls, SSL certificates, and secure passwords.
3. **Test Configurations**:
   a. Validate web and database server configurations in a staging environment before deploying.
4. **Monitor Server Performance**:
   a. Use tools like top, htop, or monitoring dashboards for insights.
5. **Automate Backups**:
   a. Schedule periodic backups and verify their integrity.

By following these guidelines, administrators can ensure reliable and secure web and database server operations.

www.ingramcontent.com/pod-product-compliance
Lightning Source LLC
LaVergne TN
LVHW051708050326
832903LV00032B/4071